hamlyn
QuickCook

hamlyn

QuickCook
Chicken

Recipes by Emma Jane Frost

Every dish, three ways – you choose!
30 minutes | 20 minutes | 10 minutes

An Hachette UK Company
www.hachette.co.uk

First published in Great Britain in 2012 by Hamlyn,
a division of Octopus Publishing Group Ltd
Endeavour House, 189 Shaftesbury Avenue
London WC2H 8JY
www.octopusbooks.co.uk

Recipes and text by Emma Jane Frost, Nichola Palmer & Sophie Jones
Copyright © Octopus Publishing Group Ltd 2012

ISBN 978-0-60062-367-0

A CIP catalogue record for this book is available from the British Library

Printed and bound in China

10 9 8 7 6 5 4 3 2 1

Both metric and imperial measurements are given for the recipes. Use one set of
measures only, not a mixture of both.

Standard level spoon measurements are used in all recipes
1 tablespoon = 15 ml
1 teaspoon = 5 ml

Ovens should be preheated to the specified temperature. If using a fan-assisted oven,
follow the manufacturer's instructions for adjusting the time and temperature. Grills
should also be preheated.

This book includes dishes made with nuts and nut derivatives. It is advisable for
those with known allergic reactions to nuts and nut derivatives and those who may
be potentially vulnerable to these allergies, such as pregnant and nursing mothers,
invalids, the elderly, babies and children, to avoid dishes made with nuts and nut oils.

It is also prudent to check the labels of preprepared ingredients for the possible
inclusion of nut derivatives.

The Department of Health advises that eggs should not be consumed raw. This book
contains some dishes made with raw or lightly cooked eggs. It is prudent for more
vulnerable people such as pregnant and nursing mothers, invalids, the elderly, babies
and young children to avoid uncooked or lightly cooked dishes made with eggs.

Contents

Introduction

30 20 10 – Quick, Quicker, Quickest

This book offers a new and flexible approach to meal-planning for busy cooks, letting you choose the recipe option that best fits the time you have available. Inside you will find 360 dishes that will inspire and motivate you to get cooking every day of the year. All the recipes take a maximum of 30 minutes to cook. Some take as little as 20 minutes and, amazingly, many take only 10 minutes. With a bit of preparation, you can easily try out one new recipe from this book each night and slowly you will be able to build a wide and exciting portfolio of recipes to suit your needs.

How Does it Work?

Every recipe in the QuickCook series can be cooked one of three ways – a 30-minute version, a 20-minute version or a super-quick and easy 10-minute version. At the beginning of each chapter you'll find recipes listed by time. Choose a dish based on how much time you have and turn to that page.

You'll find the main recipe in the middle of the page accompanied by a beautiful photograph, as well as two time-variation recipes below.

If you enjoy your chosen dish, why not go back and cook the other time-variation options at a later date? So if you liked the 20-minute Mozzarella Chicken Melts, but only have 10 minutes to spare this time around, you'll find a way to cook it using cheat ingredients or clever shortcuts.

If you love the ingredients and flavours of the 10-minute Chicken Laksa with Noodles, why not try something more substantial, like the 20-minute Stir-Fried Chicken Noodles, or be inspired to make a more elaborate version, like the Thai Chicken Curry? Alternatively, browse through all 360 delicious recipes, find something that catches your eye – then cook the version that fits your time frame.

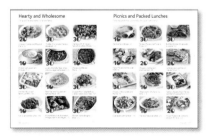

Or, for easy inspiration, turn to the gallery on pages 12–19 to get an instant overview by themes, such as Classics or Hearty and Wholesome.

QuickCook Online

To make life even easier, you can use the special code on each recipe page to email yourself a recipe card for printing, or email a text-only shopping list to your phone. Go to www.hamlynquickcook.com and enter the recipe code at the bottom of each page.

CHI-LIGH-QYZ

QuickCook Chicken

Chicken is the most widely consumed meat on the planet. It is inexpensive, quick to cook and hugely versatile, and its mild flavour makes it a favourite with people of every age.

The unending appeal of chicken as a source of protein lies in its mild flavour, which lends itself to being blended with a host of different ingredients, from the delicate tastes of Mediterranean foods, such as basil and olives, to the rich, heavily spiced stews and curries of India. This is why we find chicken in so many recipes from around the globe, and why we have been able to include so many exciting and different recipes in this book.

Think of chicken as a blank canvas to which you can add your favourite flavours. Chicken works with almost every style of cooking: Asian-style stir-fries; garlicky or herby grilled dishes; richly spiced curries; warm and cold salads; fragrant Thai coconut recipes; coq au vin and other wine-based stews; simple pasta dishes ... the opportunities for your evening meal are almost endless.

Tips and Techniques

There a few simple cooking aids that really can have an amazing effect on the time spent in the kitchen.

- A food processor and a mini chopper, are both really useful pieces of equipment which are great time-savers.

- A good vegetable peeler, garlic peeler and crusher are all great, simple little gadgets to help save time on fiddly jobs.

- Good, sharp knives make food preparation simpler and faster.

- Try cooking large amounts and then freezing in portions. This way, you'll always have a fast, ready-made, low-effort meal at your fingertips.

- Preparing ingredients in advance will save time when you come to cook the meal later on. Peel and chop vegetables for example, then keep them refrigerated in freezer bags until you need them.

A Speedy Food

Chicken appeals to cooks for many reasons, not least because it freezes exceptionally well (a chicken can be frozen with no effect on its flavour or texture for up to two years). But its unending value as an ingredient in so many dishes can be found in the speed with which it can be cooked. This book offers you an astonishing 360 recipes and variations to choose from, and every one of them can be cooked in half an hour or less. How many other satisfying and tasty foodstuffs are this easy to prepare and cook?

A whole bird, no matter how small, cannot be cooked in less than an hour of course, but the individual parts of the chicken – a wing, a leg, a thigh or a breast – should be cookable within 30 minutes. It is worth remembering that when you are buying thighs, it pays to buy them already deboned so that you can flatten the meat or cut the flesh into chunks and thereby speed up the cooking process. If the recipe requires that you keep the thighs whole, try to buy smaller thighs because the larger they are the longer they will take to cook. If small or boneless thighs are unavailable, you can speed up the cooking process by making a few fairly deep cuts into the surface of the meat. The same is true to chicken breast. Flatten or score the meat and it will cook much quicker.

When they are preparing recipes that need small pieces of chicken breast, many people choose to use mini-fillets. These tend to be extremely tender and incredibly easy to cook, so they may be worth the extra money.

With the growth in demand for ready-prepared foods, chicken can now be found in a host of different flavours. If you look in a delicatessen or the cooked meat aisle of a supermarket you can find smoked chicken breast, which is wonderful in salads and on pizzas (try our Smoked Chicken Bruschetta on page 68), Tikka-flavoured cooked chicken pieces, which are excellent in sandwiches, and other interesting flavours, including Chinese chicken, barbecue-flavoured chicken and Cajun chicken.

A Healthy Choice

Another reason why chicken breast is such a popular choice is that it contains little fat. Steamed or grilled chicken breast is one of the leanest, healthiest meats available, and even stir-fried chicken can be low in fat as long as you are careful about the amount of oil you put in the pan. In our Healthy Feasts chapter you will find a wide array of different recipes that manage to create an abundance of flavour even without a great deal of fat or salt. Remember that a dieter's delight is a cupboard full of strong flavours, such as garlic and ginger, and herbs and spices. Try the delicious Chicken Tikka Kebabs on page 260 or the palette-tingling Chicken with Cashews and Oyster Sauce on page 278.

The key to a successful low-fat diet is to mix up the flavours in your meals so that you never get bored. In the Healthy Feasts chapter we show you a few tricks, such as how 0 per cent fat Greek yogurt can be used in place of cream and butter to create moisture and flavour in many chicken dishes.

Although the wings are also technically white meat, you should be aware that they are also the fattiest part of the bird. Be careful when you are barbecuing wings: they are prone to flare up because of the amount of fat that comes out when they are cooked. Chicken thighs and legs are still lean meat in relation to meats such as beef and lamb, however, so if you are watching your calorific intake always remove the chicken skin as the majority of the fat is stored just under the skin.

A Great Choice for Family and Friends

It seems that everybody likes chicken. You can almost guarantee that when you are entertaining a large number of guests, a chicken dish will go down especially well with everyone. Real winners at parties are the Harrisa Chicken Pilaff (see page 212 in the Food for Friends chapter), which can be served warm or cold, or if you want to impress in a hurry you can't fail with our Quick Paella with Artichokes, Chorizo and Fine Beans (see page 216), and if you are hosting a special dinner party, why not try cooking the retro classic Chicken with a Tarragon Cream Sauce and Mushroom Rice (see page 214)?

Similarly, if you are cooking for a roomful of youngsters, be they three or thirteen, chicken recipes are usually well received by most guests. Try the Chicken Pesto Pasta in our Midweek Meals chapter (see page 76) for a super-successful treat or, better still, as a way of introducing children to new flavours through the medium of chicken. How many children could resist the layered Potato, Chicken, Bacon and Thyme Gratin on page 100? And they would barely notice that they've eaten a whole heap of fabulously iron-rich vegetable when you serve them up a delicious Thick Curried Coconut and Spinach Chicken Soup (see page 142 in the Family Favourites chapter).

So defrost that chicken you've got in the freezer, choose one of our gorgeous recipes and see how many smiles are in the room when your meal has been eaten. We are certain that no matter which recipe you choose from this book today, it will be a sure-fire winner with everyone.

Spicy

Turn up the heat with this selection of spicy dishes

Hoisin Chicken and Bean Sprout Wraps 42

Mexican-Style Pasta Salad 56

Spiced Chicken Naans 64

Thai Red Curry Soup 98

Paprika Chicken with Peppers 104

Oriental Chicken Mince 106

Chicken Chilli Pasta 118

Spicy Chicken Wings with Avocado Salsa 136

Tarragon Chicken Burgers Topped with Spicy Salsa 162

Chicken Chilli with Potato Wedges and Guacamole 174

Piri-Piri Stir-Fry 202

Harissa Chicken 212

Fruity

A collection of tasty recipes with fresh fruit flavours

Lemon, Mint & Chicken Skewers 70

Moroccan Fruity Chicken Stew 78

Coronation Chicken 82

Chicken Biryani 130

Simple Mango and Coconut Curry with Coriander 172

Chicken Topped with Blue Cheese and Mango Chutney 218

Chicken Apricot and Almond Tagine 220

Lime and Sweet Chilli Chicken with Sweet Potato Mash 246

Saucy Lemon Chicken with Greens 250

Spiced Roast Chicken with Lime 262

Warm Chicken, Pine Nut and Raisin Salad 266

Herby Quinoa with Lemon and Chicken 268

Classics

Eternally popular classic dishes for all the family

1 Caesar Salad with Chicken, Bacon and Parmesan 52

1 Cheesy Chicken Omelette 60

2 Pan-Fried Chicken with Garlicky Bean Mash 84

3 Potato, Chicken, Bacon and Thyme Gratin 100

2 Chicken Curry in a Hurry 110

3 Chicken, Broccoli and Cheese Bake 120

3 Roasted Chicken Thighs with Roots and Honey 128

3 Speedy Roast Chicken with Bacon and Stuffing 146

3 Chicken, Leek and Parsley Pies 154

3 Quick Coq au Vin 204

1 Chicken Minestrone 240

3 Chicken Ratatouille 258

Taste of the Med

Recipes to savour the flavours of the Mediterranean

Souvlaki 38

Chicken Pesto Pasta 76

Basil, Ricotta and Sun-Dried Tomato Chicken 94

Tomato, Chicken, Pepper and Olive Tuscan-Style Tarts 132

Chicken Parmigiana 180

Greek-Style Chicken Thighs with Olives and Green Beans 182

Grilled Gazpacho Chicken Salad 186

Chicken and Fennel Risotto with Vermouth 194

Chicken Koftas 214

Quick Paella with Artichokes, Chorizo and Green Beans 216

Chicken Roasted with Lemon, Olives and Saffron 274

Yogurt Chicken with Greek Salad 276

Hearty and Wholesome

Filling and healthy dishes for all the family

Chicken, Chorizo and Broccoli Pasta 88

Thai Red Curry with Chicken Meatballs 90

Chicken with Potatoes, Spinach and Blue Cheese 112

Chicken and Sweetcorn Chowder 114

Smoky Cannellini Bean Stew with Sausages and Chicken 122

Chicken and Boston Beans 134

Chicken, Bacon and Mushroom Pie 138

Thick Curried Coconut and Spinach Soup 142

Chicken Pesto Meatballs in Tomato Sauce with Pasta 158

Lentil and Chicken Stew 164

Roasted Beetroot, Butternut Wedges and Thyme Thighs 222

Chicken and Aubergine Bake 242

Picnics and Packed Lunches

Tasty recipes to transport easily when you're on the run

Chicken Salsa Wraps 24

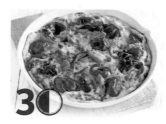

Fennel, Chicken and Tomato Pizza 34

Buffalo Chicken Wings with Coleslaw 44

Cajun Chicken and Avocado Melt 46

Chicken, Chorizo and Sage Skewers 48

Chicken, Basil and Goats' Cheese Panini 54

Chicken, Feta and Spinach Pasties 96

Simple Warm Chicken Liver Pâté 188

Chicken, Spinach, Onion Chutney and Goats' Cheese Tart 192

Panzanella with Chicken 196

Chicken Couscous Salad 248

Mixed Mushroom, Herb and Chicken Fritatta 254

Takeaway Treats

Recreate your favourite takeaway dishes at home

Curried Chicken Samosas 26

Jerk Chicken and Pepper Stir-Fry 32

Chicken Nachos 50

Smoky Barbecue Chicken Pizza 58

Chicken and Rustic Chips 108

Simple Chicken Korma 148

Fajitas 168

Chicken Tacos 234

Chicken Pilau with Cauliflower, Spinach and Green Beans 244

Baked Chicken and Prawn Spring Rolls 256

Chicken Tikka Kebabs with Red Onion Relish 260

Chicken with Cashews and Oyster Sauce 278

Batch Cooking

Recipes that can be made in advance and eaten later

3 Chicken Quesadillas with Coriander and Chilli 62

2 Smoked Chicken Bruschetta 68

1 Chicken Satay 92

3 Crispy Salt and Pepper Chicken Thighs 102

3 Chicken, Bacon, Vegetable and Cheese Layers 144

3 Barbecue Poussin Pieces with Corn and Chilli Salsa 150

1 Warm Chicken Ciabatta with Salsa and Rocket 152

2 Wholemeal Chicken Gougons with Lemon Mayonnaise 156

3 Sticky Soy-Glazed Drumsticks 170

2 Sesame and Thyme Skewers with Spiced Chickpea Mash 190

3 Chicken Drumstick Jambalaya 236

2 Spanish Chicken and Potato Stew 252

QuickCook
Light Bites

Recipes listed by cooking time

10

10 Chicken Salsa Wraps

Serves 4

200 g (7 oz) fresh tomato salsa
4 soft flour tortillas
250 g (8 oz) ready-cooked barbecue-flavoured chicken, chopped
¼ small red cabbage, shredded
2 carrots, coarsely grated
4 spring onions, cut into fine strips
150 ml (¼ pint) soured cream
green salad, to serve

· Spoon the tomato salsa on to the tortillas and spread it evenly. Place a quarter of the chicken in the centre of each one with some of the cabbage, carrots and spring onions.

· Top with soured cream and roll up. Cut in half and serve with a green salad.

 ### 2 Chicken Salsa Jackets

Cook 4 baking potatoes, each about 150 g (5 oz), in a microwave oven for 10–15 minutes or until soft. Meanwhile, mix together 200 g (7 oz) cooked and chopped barbecue-flavoured chicken, ¼ small shredded red cabbage, 2 coarsely grated carrots and 4 chopped spring onions. Stir in 4 tablespoons mayonnaise and season with salt and pepper. Cut open the potatoes, fill with the chicken mixture and spoon ready-made tomato salsa on top.

 ### 3 Balsamic Chicken Wraps

Thinly slice 3 boneless, skinless chicken breasts and coat in a mixture of 2 tablespoons balsamic vinegar, 2 tablespoons olive oil and 1 crushed garlic clove. Season with salt and pepper. Cook the chicken, in batches, on a hot griddle or frying pan for 1–2 minutes on each side until cooked through. Place on warmed soft flour tortillas with 200 g (7 oz) tomato salsa, ¼ small shredded red cabbage, 2 grated carrots and 4 spring onions, cut into strips. Top with soured cream, roll up and serve.

3 Curried Chicken Samosas

Serves 4

200 g (7 oz) potatoes, finely chopped

100 g (3½ oz) frozen mixed vegetables (such as peas, sweetcorn and carrots)

200 g (7 oz) cooked chicken, chopped

1 tablespoon medium curry paste

1 tablespoon mango chutney

8 sheets of filo pastry, thawed if frozen, halved lengthways

1 tablespoon sunflower oil

1 tablespoon poppy seeds

mango chutney, to serve

- Cook the potatoes in lightly salted boiling water for 5 minutes, adding the frozen vegetables towards the end so that they thaw.

- Meanwhile, mix together the chicken, curry paste and mango chutney. Drain the vegetables, add to the chicken and mix well.

- Place 2 tablespoons of the mixture in the corner of ½ sheet of filo pastry. Fold the end of the pastry over the filling to make a triangle, then continue folding along the pastry, keeping the triangular shape until the pastry is used up. Place on a baking sheet and repeat with remaining filling and pastry to make 8 samosas.

- Brush the tops of the samosas with oil, sprinkle with poppy seeds and bake in the preheated oven, 200°C (400°F), Gas Mark 6, for 15 minutes until golden and crisp. Serve with mango chutney.

---

1 **Curried Chicken and Rice**

Mix together 250 g (8 oz) packet ready-cooked basmati rice with 1 tablespoon medium curry paste and 1 tablespoon mango chutney. Add 200 g (7 oz) cooked chopped chicken and 125 g (4 oz) frozen mixed vegetables. Heat in a microwave oven for 5 minutes until hot. Serve with extra mango chutney and poppadoms.

2 **Curried Chicken Puffs**

Cut a sheet of ready-rolled puff pastry into 4 squares. In a bowl mix together 200 g (7 oz) cooked chopped chicken, 1 tablespoon medium curry paste and 1 tablespoon mango chutney. Add 200 g (7 oz) finely chopped potatoes and a handful of canned sweetcorn kernels. Place the filling on one triangular half of each pastry square. Brush the edges with a little beaten egg and fold the pastry over to make triangles, pressing down well to seal. Place on a baking sheet, brush with egg and bake in a preheated oven, 200°C (400°F), Gas Mark 6, for 10 minutes or until well risen and golden. Serve warm with mango chutney.

30 Creamy Herby Chicken with Mushrooms on Bagels

Serves 4

4 bagels, halved

25 g (1 oz) ready-made garlic butter, softened

2 tablespoons olive oil

1 small onion, chopped

2 skinless chicken breast fillets, sliced

175 g (6 oz) chestnut mushrooms, quartered

2 tablespoons sherry

200 ml (7 fl oz) crème fraîche

2 tablespoons chopped parsley

salt and pepper

- Place the bagel halves, cut sides up on a baking sheet, spread over the garlic butter and bake in a preheated oven, 190°C (375°F), Gas Mark 5, for 10–15 minutes until crisp.

- Meanwhile, heat the oil in a frying pan, add the onion and cook for 3 minutes. Add the chicken and cook for 5 minutes. Add the mushrooms cook for a further 5 minutes until tender. Add the sherry and allow to bubble, then stir in the crème fraîche and parsley and season with salt and pepper. Simmer, stirring, adding a little water if the mixture is too thick. Spoon over the baked bagels and serve.

 **Creamy Chicken and Mushrooms on Toast** Fry 125 g (4 oz) sliced mushrooms in 25 g (1 oz) ready-made garlic butter for 3 minutes until tender. Stir in 400 g (13 oz) can of chicken in cream sauce and heat, stirring, for a few minutes until hot. Stir in 1 tablespoon chopped parsley and spoon over hot buttered toast to serve.

 Garlic Baked Mushrooms with Chicken Put 4 large portobello mushrooms, stalk sides up, on a baking sheet. Dot with 25 g (1 oz) ready-made garlic butter, season with salt and pepper and bake in a preheated oven, 200°C (400°F), Gas Mark 6, for 15 minutes until tender. Meanwhile, fry 1 small onion and 2 chopped skinless chicken breast fillets in 1 tablespoon olive oil for 5 minutes. Stir in 200 ml (7 fl oz) crème fraîche and 2 tablespoons chopped parsley. Season with salt and pepper and simmer for 5 minutes, adding a little water if the mixture becomes too thick. Spoon over the baked garlicky mushrooms to serve.

Chicken, Courgette and Bacon Kebabs

Serves 4

16 rashers unsmoked streaky
bacon
2 courgettes, each cut into
8 chunks
3 skinless chicken breast fillets,
each cut into 8 pieces
1 tablespoon sunflower oil
2 tablespoons clear honey
1 tablespoon wholegrain mustard
sweetcorn and peas, to serve

- Stretch each bacon rasher with the back of a knife. Cut each rasher in half and wrap around a piece of courgette. Thread on to 8 skewers, alternating the courgettes with pieces of chicken.

- Place the kebabs on a foil-lined grill pan. Warm the oil, honey and mustard together in a small pan, brush over the kebabs and cook under a preheated medium grill for 10 minutes, turning occasionally and brushing with any remaining honey mixture until the bacon is crisp and the chicken is cooked. Serve with sweetcorn and peas.

 Chicken, Bacon and Courgette Baguette Cut 2 courgettes into slices lengthways and place on a foil-lined grill pan. Brush the courgettes with a little oil, honey and mustard and grill together with 4 bacon rashers for about 5 minutes until the courgettes are tender and the bacon is crisp. Cut a baguette into 4 pieces and cut in half lengthways. Butter and fill with 250 g (8 oz) cooked sliced chicken and the courgettes and bacon.

Chicken, Bacon and Courgette Kebabs with Sweetcorn Fritters Prepare the kebabs as above. Put 4 tablespoons self-raising flour in a bowl with a pinch of salt. Add 2 eggs and mix to make a smooth batter. Drain 400 g (13 oz) can sweetcorn and add to the batter. Heat 2 tablepoons sunflower oil in a large frying pan, add spoonfuls of the mixture and cook for 2 minutes until set and golden underneath. Turn over and cook for a further 2 minutes. Repeat with remaining mixture and serve with the kebabs.

30 Jerk Chicken and Pepper Stir-Fry

Serves 4

1 tablespoon sunflower oil
8 chicken drumsticks
1 red pepper, cored, deseeded
  and cut into chunks
1 green pepper, cored, deseeded
  and cut into chunks
125 g (4 oz) sugar snap peas
1 mango, stone removed and
  flesh chopped
juice of 1 lime
600 ml (1 pint) rich chicken stock
1 tablespoon sunflower oil

For the jerk paste

1 red onion, roughly chopped
1 teaspoon dried thyme
½ teaspoon ground allspice
½ teaspoon ground cinnamon
1 bell chilli, roughly chopped
salt and pepper

- To make the jerk paste, put all the paste ingredients in a small food processor or blender and process to make a smooth paste.

- Cut a few slashes across the thickest part of each drumstick. Rub the paste over the drumsticks, pushing it into the slashes.

- Heat the oil in a large deep frying pan. Add the chicken drumsticks and peppers and fry over a high heat for 5 minutes, turning occasionally. Add the sugar snap peas, mango, lime juice and stock and bring to the boil. Reduce the heat and cover and simmer for 15 minutes, turning the chicken occasionally until cooked through. Serve with rice.

 Jerk Chicken Burgers

Slice 2 skinless chicken breast fillets in half horizontally. Season and fry in 1 tablespoon sunflower oil for 5 minutes, turning once, until cooked through. Serve in burger buns with ready-made jerk sauce and crisp lettuce.

 Jerk Chicken with Rice and Peas

Heat 400 ml (14 fl oz) can coconut milk in a pan with 450 ml (¾ pint) water. Add 175 g (6 oz) easy-cook long grain rice, 400 g (13 oz) can rinsed and drained kidney beans and 1 teaspoon dried thyme. Bring to the boil, reduce the heat, cover and simmer for 15 minutes until the rice is tender and most of the liquid has been absorbed. Meanwhile, toss 4 sliced skinless chicken breast fillets in 1 tablespoon jerk seasoning mix. Stir-fry the chicken in 1 tablespoon sunflower oil for 5 minutes until cooked through. Serve with rice and peas and with wedges of lime.

30 Fennel, Chicken and Tomato Pizza

Serves 2

2 tablespoons olive oil
1 small onion, sliced
1 garlic clove, crushed
3 tomatoes, chopped
pinch of sugar
1 tablespoon tomato purée
145 g (4½ oz) pizza base mix
1 small head of fennel, thinly
  sliced
125 g (4 oz) cooked chicken,
  chopped
8 cherry tomatoes, halved
150 g (5 oz) mozzarella cheese,
  sliced
salt and pepper

• Heat the olive oil in a frying pan, add the onion, garlic and fennel and cook for 3 minutes. Add the tomatoes, sugar and tomato purée and simmer for 5 minutes until the mixture is soft and pulpy. Season with salt and pepper.

• Meanwhile, make the pizza base according to the instructions on the packet. Knead lightly until smooth, shape into a ball and roll out thinly to a circle about 30 cm (12 inches) across. Place on a baking sheet.

• Spread the tomato and fennel sauce over the pizza base and scatter over the chicken and cherry tomatoes. Arrange the mozzarella on top and bake in a preheated oven, 220°C (425°F), Gas Mark 7, for 15 minutes until crisp and golden.

1 Chicken and Fennel Pizza

Top a garlic and herb flat bread with ready-made pizza topping sauce, thin slices from a small fennel head, and 125 g (4 oz) chopped cooked chicken. Arrange 150 g (5 oz) sliced mozzarella cheese on top and bake in a preheated oven, 220°C (425°F) Gas Mark 7, for 10 minutes.

2 Fennel, Chicken and Tomato Pasta

Heat 2 tablespoons olive oil in a pan, add 1 chopped onion, 1 crushed garlic clove, 250 g (8 oz) chopped cooked chicken and 1 small, chopped head of fennel. Cook for 3 minutes, then add 3 chopped tomatoes and 150 ml (¼ pint) passata. Season with salt and pepper and stir in a handful of black olives. Serve with freshly cooked pasta.

Parmesan Chicken Escalopes

Serves 4

2 skinless chicken breast fillets,
   halved horizontally
2 tablespoons plain flour
1 egg, beaten
125 g (4 oz) fresh ciabatta
   breadcrumbs
75 g (3 oz) freshly grated
   Parmesan cheese
3 tablespoons sunflower oil
4 small baguettes, cut in half
   lengthways
4 tablespoons mayonnaise
4 small handfuls mixed salad
   leaves
salt and pepper

· Place the chicken halves between 2 pieces of clingfilm and
  beat with a rolling pin to flatten slightly. Put the flour on
  a plate and the egg in a dish. On a separate plate mix
  together the breadcrumbs and Parmesan and season with
  salt and pepper.

· Lightly coat each piece of chicken in flour, shaking off any
  excess, dip into the beaten egg and coat in the breadcrumb
  mixture, pressing them on firmly.

· Heat the oil in a large frying pan, add the chicken and cook
  for about 5 minutes, turning once, until golden, crisp and
  cooked through.

· Fill the baguette pieces with mayonnaise, salad leaves and
  the hot chicken.

---

1 Chicken Caesar Baguette

Stir-fry 2 skinless chicken
breasts, cut into strips, in
2 tablespoons sunflower oil for
about 5 minutes or until cooked
through. Pile into pieces of
French bread with mixed salad
leaves and a drizzle of Caesar
salad dressing.

3 Baked Pesto Parmesan Chicken with Sweet Potato Wedges

Cut 4 scrubbed sweet potatoes
into wedges. Toss in 4
tablespoons olive oil and season
with salt and pepper. Spread out
over a baking sheet and bake in a
preheated oven, 220°C (425°F),
Gas Mark 7, for 25 minutes,
turning occasionally, until golden
and tender. Meanwhile, cut
2 skinless chicken breast fillets in
half horizontally. Spread with
pesto sauce and sprinkle with
125 g (4 oz) fresh white
breadcrumbs mixed with 75 g
(3 oz) freshly grated Parmesan
cheese. Place on a baking sheet
and drizzle over 3 tablespoons
sunflower oil. Bake in the oven
with the sweet potatoes for
15 minutes until crisp and cooked
through. Serve with mayonnaise
and mixed salad leaves.

3 Souvlaki

Serves 4

3 tablespoons olive oil
3 tablespoons red wine
1 teaspoon dried oregano
finely grated rind and juice of
   1 lemon
1 garlic clove, crushed
4 skinless chicken breast fillets,
   each cut into strips
4 pitta breads, warmed and split
   open
salt and pepper

To serve

cabbage, shredded
cucumber, chopped
tomato, chopped
chilli sauce

· In a large bowl mix together the olive oil, wine, oregano, lemon rind and juice and garlic. Season with salt and pepper, add the chicken, mix well and leave to marinate for 15 minutes.

· Thread the chicken on to skewers and place on a foil-lined grill pan. Cook under a preheated hot grill for 8–10 minutes, turning occasionally, until the chicken is cooked and beginning to char at the edges.

· Slide the chicken off the skewers into the warm pitta bread and add some shredded cabbage, chopped cucumber, chopped tomato and a dash of chilli sauce.

 Hot Chicken and Hummus Pitta Pockets Stir-fry 220 g (7½ oz) mini-chicken fillets in 1 tablespoon olive oil with ½ teaspoon dried oregano, 1 teaspoon garlic paste and the grated rind of ½ lemon for 5 minutes until cooked through. Warm 4 pitta breads, cut in half widthways and open out to form pockets, and serve the chicken inside with 4 tablespoons ready-made hummus and crisp cos (romaine) lettuce.

 Pan-Fried Lemon Chicken with Courgettes Thinly slice 4 skinless chicken breast fillets and toss in a mixture of 3 tablespoons olive oil, 3 tablespoons red wine, 1 teaspoon dried oregano, the finely grated rind and juice of 1 lemon and 2 crushed garlic cloves. Leave to marinate for 15 minutes. Pan-fry the chicken in a hot frying pan with 2 tablespoons olive oil and 2 courgettes cut into thin sticks for 5 minutes until golden. Add the marinade and cook for a few minutes to reduce slightly. Serve with rice.

30 Smoked Chicken, Asparagus and Blue Cheese Calzone

Serves 2

175 g (6 oz) asparagus spears, trimmed and cut into 2 cm (1 inch) pieces

145 g (4½ oz) pizza base mix

1 smoked cooked chicken breast, sliced

125 g (4 oz) Roquefort cheese, crumbled

rocket leaves, to serve

- Cook the asparagus in lightly salted boiling water for 3 minutes until just tender, then drain.

- Meanwhile, make the pizza base mix according to the instructions on the packet. Knead lightly until smooth then roll out thinly to make a large circle, about 30 cm (12 inches) across, then place on a baking sheet.

- Scatter the chicken, asparagus and crumbled cheese over half the dough, leaving a 1 cm (½ inch) border. Brush the edges with water, fold the dough over to cover the filling, pressing the edges firmly to seal. Bake in a preheated oven, 220°C (425°F), Gas Mark 7, for 15 minutes until crisp and golden. Serve warm with rocket leaves.

 1 **Smoked Chicken, Asparagus and Blue Cheese Salad** Put 150 g (5 oz) mixed salad leaves in a bowl. Add 1 sliced smoked chicken breast, 175 g (6 oz) lightly cooked asparagus spears and a handful of pine nuts. Drizzle with ready-made blue cheese salad dressing and toss lightly to mix.

 2 **Smoked Chicken and Asparagus Tarts** Cook 175 g (6 oz) trimmed and halved asparagus spears in lightly salted boiling water for 3 minutes, then drain. Unroll half a sheet of ready-rolled puff pastry and cut it into 2 rectangles. Place on a baking sheet and divide the topping between the 2 tarts, each with half 1 sliced smoked chicken breast, the asparagus and 125 g (4 oz) crumbled Roquefort cheese. Bake in a preheated oven, 220°C (425°F), Gas Mark 7, for 10–15 minutes until well risen and golden.

 # Hoisin Chicken and Bean Sprout Wraps

Serves 4

1 tablespoon vegetable oil

3 skinless chicken breast fillets, cut into strips

2 tablespoons hoisin sauce, plus extra for dipping

½ teaspoon ginger paste

2 teaspoons dark soy sauce

8 rice flour pancakes (the sort used for crispy duck)

125 g (4 oz) bean sprouts

4 spring onions, cut into thin strips

¼ cucumber, cut into thin strips

- Heat the oil in a wok or frying pan, add the chicken and cook over a high heat for 5 minutes or until cooked through. Add the hoisin sauce, ginger paste and soy sauce and cook, stirring, until the sauce is sticky and coats the chicken. Remove from the heat.

- Warm the pancakes in a microwave oven or in a low oven according to the instructions on the packet. Divide the the bean sprouts, spring onions and cucumber among the pancakes, top with chicken and roll up. Serve with extra hoisin sauce for dipping.

Hoisin Chicken Rice Noodle Salad

Coat about 400 g (13 oz) mini-chicken breast fillets in 125 g (4 oz) packet hoisin and garlic stir-fry sauce. Stir-fry in 1 tablespoon sunflower oil for about 5 minutes until cooked. Meanwhile, soak 200 g (7 oz) vermicelli rice noodles in boiling water for a few minutes until softened. Drain, mix with the cooked chicken and 200 g (7 oz) oriental salad mix.

Hoisin Chicken Parcels

In a large bowl mix together 2 tablespoons hoisin sauce, ½ teaspoon ginger paste and 2 teaspoons dark soy sauce. Add 2 thinly sliced skinless chicken breast fillets, 4 spring onions, cut into strips, 125 g (4 oz) bean sprouts and 1 large carrot, cut into strips. Divide the mixture among 4 large squares of double thickness greaseproof paper. Fold the paper over the filling, twisting the edges to form a parcel. Place on a baking sheet and cook in a preheated oven, 200°C (400°F), Gas Mark 6, for 20 minutes. Serve with freshly cooked noodles.

30 Buffalo Chicken Wings with Coleslaw

Serves 4

2 tablespoons clear honey

5 tablespoons tomato ketchup

2 teaspoons English mustard

2 teaspoons Worcestershire
  sauce

½–1 teaspoon hot chilli sauce

2 tablespoons sunflower oil

1 kg (2 lb) chicken wings

For the coleslaw

4 tablespoons mayonnaise

2 tablespoons lemon juice

375 g (12 oz) white cabbage,
  finely shredded

1 small red onion, finely shredded

1 medium carrot, coarsely grated

1 tablespoon chopped parsley

pepper

- In a large bowl mix together the honey, ketchup, mustard, Worcestershire sauce, chilli sauce and oil. Add the chicken wings and mix well to coat.

- Put the chicken wings on a large, foil-lined baking sheet and bake in a preheated oven, 200°C (400°F), Gas Mark 6, for 25 minutes, turning occasionally and brushing with any remaining sauce in the bowl, until cooked through.

- Meanwhile, make the coleslaw. Mix together the ingredients and season with pepper. Serve the chicken wings with the coleslaw on the side.

10 Spicy Chicken and Corn

Reheat 750 g (1 lb 8 oz) ready-cooked and spicy-flavoured chicken wings in a microwave oven according to the instructions on the packet. Serve with chunks of corn on the cob that have been cooked in lightly salted boiling water for 5–8 minutes until tender. Sprinkle with chilli flakes and dot with butter to serve.

20 Barbecue Chicken with Blue Cheese

Dip and Celery Cut 4 skinless chicken breast fillets into strips. Coat in a mixture of 1 tablespoon clear honey, 2½ tablespoons tomato ketchup, 1 teaspoon English mustard, 1 teaspoon Worcestershire sauce, a dash of hot chilli sauce and 1 tablespoon sunflower oil. Spread the chicken pieces over a foil-lined grill pan and grill, turning occasionally, for 5–10 minutes or until cooked through. Meanwhile, mash together with a fork 150 ml (¼ pint) soured cream and 50 g (2 oz) crumbled blue cheese. Serve the chicken with the blue cheese dip and raw celery sticks.

Cajun Chicken and Avocado Melt

Serves 2

1 small ciabatta loaf, halved
  lengthways
2 tablespoons tomato chutney
2 tomatoes, sliced
100 g ready-cooked Cajun-spiced
  chicken breast, sliced
1 small avocado, sliced
150 g (5 oz) mozzarella cheese,
  drained and sliced

- Put the ciabatta halves, cut side down, on a foil-lined grill pan and toast under a preheated medium grill for a few minutes until crisp and hot. Turn over the bread and spread with the tomato chutney. Arrange the tomato slices on top, followed by the chicken, avocado and finally the mozzarella.

- Place under the grill and cook for 5 minutes or until the cheese has melted and the topping is hot.

---

2 Cajun Chicken Burgers

Cut 2 skinless chicken breast fillets in half horizontally and sprinkle over 1 teaspoon Cajun seasoning mix. Fry in 1 tablespoon sunflower oil for 5 minutes, turning once, until golden and cooked through. Place on toasted burger buns with slices of tomato and avocado. Serve topped with tomato salsa and soured cream.

3 Cajun Chicken 'Rarebit'

Mix together 200 g (7 oz) grated mature Cheddar cheese, 1 teaspoon Cajun seasoning mix, a pinch of cayenne pepper, ½ beaten egg and 1 tablespoon beer. Toast 2 large slices of crusty bread on both sides, top with 1 cooked and sliced chicken breast and 2 sliced tomatoes. Spread the cheese mixture over the top and cook under the grill until golden and bubbling.

Chicken, Chorizo and Sage Skewers

Serves 4

4 skinless chicken thigh fillets,
  each cut into 4 pieces
4 small cooking chorizo, halved
12 sage leaves
1 tablespoon olive oil
2 teaspoon wholegrain mustard

To serve

baby spinach leaves
crusty bread

- Thread the chicken, chorizo and sage leaves on to 4 metal skewers. Mix together the olive oil and wholegrain mustard and brush over the skewers.

- Cook on a hot griddle pan or under a preheated hot grill for 10–15 minutes, turning occasionally and brushing with more mustard mixture until the chicken and chorizo are cooked.

- Slide the chicken and chorizo off the skewers and serve with baby spinach leaves and crusty bread.

---

10 Chicken and Chorizo Pasta

Cook 375 g (12 oz) quick-cook pasta shapes in a pan of lightly salted boiling water for 5–8 minutes or until tender. Meanwhile, fry 75 g (3 oz) sliced chorizo in a dry frying pan for 2 minutes. Add 350 g (11½ oz) tomato pasta sauce from a jar and 175 g (6 oz) cooked chopped chicken. Heat through, drain the pasta and add to the sauce. Mix well and serve with freshly grated Parmesan cheese.

30 Quick Roast Chicken with Chorizo and Potatoes

Toss 4 halved skinless chicken thigh fillets and 8 small cooking chorizo (weighing 75 g/3 oz each) in a mixture of 1 tablespoon olive oil and 2 teaspoons wholegrain mustard. Place in a roasting tin with 400 g (13 oz) baby new potatoes and 3 whole unpeeled garlic cloves. Drizzle with 2 more tablespoons olive oil, season with salt and pepper and bake in a preheated oven, 200°C (400°F), Gas Mark 6, for 25 minutes until golden and tender. Meanwhile, fry 1 chopped onion and 1 crushed garlic clove in 1 tablespoon olive oil for 5 minutes until softened. Add 200 g (7 oz) can chopped tomatoes and 1 tablespoon tomato purée and simmer, stirring occasionally, until thickened. Serve the sauce with the chicken, chorizo and potatoes.

3 Chicken Nachos

Serves 4

6 soft corn tortillas
1 tablespoon sunflower oil
½ teaspoon sea salt flakes
3 tomatoes, finely chopped
1 red chilli, deseeded and finely
  chopped
1 tablespoon chopped fresh
  coriander
juice of 1 lime
200 g (7 oz) cooked chicken,
  chopped
50 g (2 oz) sliced Jalapeño
  peppers from a jar, drained
75 g (3 oz) Cheddar cheese,
  grated
salt and pepper
fresh coriander leaves, to garnish
150 ml (¼ pint) soured cream,
  to serve

- Brush the tortillas with oil, sprinkle with sea salt and cut into triangles. Spread them out on 2 baking sheets and bake in a preheated oven, 190°C (375°F), Gas Mark 5, for 8–10 minutes until crisp. Cool on a wire rack while you make the salsa.

- Mix together the tomatoes, chilli, coriander and lime juice. Season with salt and pepper.

- Sprinkle the chicken over the baked tortillas with the Jalapeno peppers and chopped tomato mixture. Scatter the grated Cheddar over the top and return to the oven for 3–4 minutes for the cheese to melt. Garnish with coriander leaves and serve with soured cream.

1 Quick-Assembly Nachos

Spread 200 g (7 oz) tortilla chips over the base of an ovenproof dish. Sprinkle over 200 g (7 oz) chopped cooked chicken and 50 g (2 oz) sliced Jalapeño peppers from a jar. Dot with spoonfuls of ready-made salsa and sprinkle over 75 g (3 oz) grated Cheddar cheese. Place under a medium hot grill for 5 minutes until the cheese has melted. Serve with soured cream.

2 Burritos

Mix together 3 finely chopped tomatoes, 1 finely chopped red chilli, 1 tablespoon chopped fresh coriander and the juice of 1 lime. Spoon the mixture down the centre of 4 soft flour tortillas. Top with spoonfuls of ready-made guacamole, 200 g (7 oz) chopped cooked chicken and 50 g (2 oz) sliced Jalapeno peppers from a jar. Fold a 2 cm (1 inch) strip of tortilla over at the bottom of the filling, turn the tortilla 90 degrees and roll up like a pancake. Secure with a cocktail stick.

10 Caesar Salad with Chicken, Bacon and Parmesan

Serves 4

½ ciabatta loaf, cubed

2 tablespoons olive oil

1 cos (romaine) lettuce, leaves separated

200 g (7 oz) cooked chicken, chopped

75 g (3 oz) cooked crispy bacon rashers, broken into pieces

6 tablespoons ready-made Caesar salad dressing

25 g (1 oz) Parmesan cheese shavings

· Place the ciabatta cubes on a foil-lined grill pan and drizzle over the olive oil. Toast under a preheated medium grill for about 5 minutes, turning occasionally, until golden and crisp.

· Meanwhile, roughly tear the lettuce leaves and place in a salad bowl with the chicken and most of the bacon pieces.

· Add the toasted bread cubes and salad dressing and toss well to mix. Sprinkle over the reserved bacon pieces and the Parmesan shavings. Serve straight away.

 Chicken Caesar with Garlicky Croutons Cut ½ ciabatta loaf into cubes. Mix 1 crushed garlic clove and 4 tablespoons olive oil and toss the cubes in the oil. Spread on a baking sheet and bake in a preheated oven, 200°C (400°F), Gas Mark 6, for 10 minutes until crisp. Add to a bowl of torn cos lettuce leaves, chopped cooked chicken and crispy bacon pieces tossed in ready-made Caesar salad dressing.

 Caesar Salad with Homemade Dressing Cut ½ ciabatta loaf into cubes, place on a baking sheet and drizzle over 2 tablespoons olive oil. Bake in a preheated oven, 200°C (400°F), Gas Mark 6, for 15 minutes until crisp and golden. Meanwhile, make the dressing. In a bowl mix together 3 tablespoons mayonnaise, 25 g (1 oz) freshly grated Parmesan cheese, 1 tablespoon lemon juice, 2 tablespoons water, a dash of Worcestershire sauce and 1 finely chopped anchovy fillet from a can. Put the torn leaves of 1 cos lettuce in a bowl with 200 g (7 oz) cooked chopped chicken, 75 g (3 oz) cooked crispy bacon broken into pieces and the bread cubes. Toss together with the dressing and serve.

20 Chicken, Basil and Goats' Cheese Panini

Serves 4

4 tablespoons pesto
1 tablespoon olive oil
4 panini rolls or 4 part-baked
  baguettes, halved
2 cooked chicken breasts, sliced
125 g (4 oz) sun-dried tomatoes
  in oil, drained
200 g (7 oz) goats' cheese, sliced
handful of fresh basil leaves

- Mix together the pesto and oil and brush over the cut side of the bottom halves of the panini rolls or baguettes. Top with the sliced chicken, sun-dried tomatoes, goats' cheese and basil. Cover with the top half of the rolls or baguettes.

- Cook in a sandwich toaster or panini grill for about 5 minutes until the bread is crisp and filling is hot. Alternatively, cook in a hot pan or griddle, pressing the rolls down firmly. Turn and cook on the other side.

 Chicken and Goats' Cheese Salad

Mix together a 100 g (3½ oz) bag of mixed salad leaves, 2 cooked sliced chicken breasts, 125 g (4 oz) chopped sun-dried tomatoes, 200 g (7 oz) sliced goats' cheese and a handful of black olives. Mix 1 tablespoon pesto with 1 tablespoon olive oil and drizzle over the dressing to serve.

 Chicken and Goats' Cheese Pizza

Spread 4 tablespoons tomato pizza topping sauce over a large ready-made pizza base. Top with 2 cooked and sliced chicken breasts, 125 g (4 oz) sliced goats' cheese and a handful of black olives. Drizzle over 1 tablespoon pesto mixed with 1 tablespoon olive oil and bake in a preheated oven, 200°C (400°F), Gas Mark 6, for 15 minutes or until the base is crisp and the topping is hot.

30 Mexican-Style Pasta Salad

Serves 4

250 g (8 oz) pasta shapes, such
as twists
1 red pepper, cored, deseeded
and halved
1 orange pepper, cored, deseeded
and halved
200 g (7 oz) cooked Cajun-style
chicken, cut into bite-sized
pieces
220 g (7½ oz) can mixed chilli beans
1 avocado, chopped
handful of fresh coriander leaves,
roughly chopped

For the dressing

150 ml (¼ pint) soured cream
finely grated rind and juice of
1 lime
½ teaspoon Cajun seasoning mix

- Cook the pasta in lightly salted boiling water for about
  10 minutes until just tender. Drain, rinse under cold running
  water and drain again.

- Meanwhile, put the peppers under a hot grill for 8–10
  minutes, turning once until softened and the skin is
  beginning to char. Transfer the peppers to a bowl, cover
  with clingfilm and leave for 5 minutes.

- Make the dressing. Mix together the soured cream, lime
  rind and juice and Cajun seasoning.

- Transfer the drained pasta to a large salad bowl. Add the
  cooked chicken, beans, avocado and coriander. Remove the
  skins from the peppers, roughly chop the flesh and add to
  the salad. Drizzle over the dressing and lightly toss together.

 **Mexican-Style
Open Sandwich**

Top 4 slices of rustic wholemeal
bread with some slices of
cooked Cajun-style chicken,
sliced tomatoes, sliced avocado,
fresh coriander leaves and
soured cream dressing.

 **Fruity Mexican
Chicken Salad**

Cook 250 g (8 oz) pasta shapes
in lightly salted boiling water for
10 minutes until just tender.
Drain, rinse under running cold
water and drain again. Mix the
cooked pasta with 200 g (7 oz)
cooked Cajun-style chicken,
125 g (4 oz) roasted red peppers
from a jar, 1 chopped mango and
a handful of fresh coriander
leaves. Serve with the soured
cream dressing as above.

30 Smoky Barbecue Chicken Pizza

Serves 4

250 g (8 oz) plain flour
½ teaspoon salt
1 teaspoon bicarbonate of soda
pinch of sugar
25 g (1 oz) cold butter
150 ml (¼ pint) buttermilk or
  natural yogurt
4 tablespoons tomato pizza
  topping sauce
250 g (8 oz) cooked chicken,
  chopped
2 tablespoons smoky barbecue
  sauce
125 g (4 oz) roasted peppers from
  a jar, chopped
150 g (5 oz) mozzarella cheese,
  sliced

- Sift the flour into a bowl with the salt, bicarbonate of soda and sugar. Coarsely grate the butter into the mixture. Stir well to break up any clumps of butter, add the buttermilk or yogurt and mix to a soft dough.

- Knead the dough lightly until smooth, shape into a ball and pat out with your hands to a large circle about 30 cm (12 inches) across. Place on a baking sheet.

- Spread the topping sauce over the dough, leaving a small border around the edge. Mix together the chicken and barbecue sauce and spread over the pizza. Arrange the peppers and mozzarella on top and bake in a preheated oven, 200°C (400°F), Gas Mark 6, for 15 minutes until the base is cooked and the topping is golden.

 Barbecue Chicken and Sweetcorn Pizza Muffins Cut 4 muffins in half, put them on a foil-lined grill pan and toast under the grill on both sides. Chop 250 g (8 oz) cooked chicken and drain 200 g (7 oz) can sweetcorn kernels. Mix the chicken and sweetcorn with 3 tablespoons smoky barbecue sauce. Spoon on to the toasted muffins, sprinkle with 125 g (4 oz) grated mature Cheddar cheese and cook under the grill until the cheese is melted and bubbling.

Thin and Crispy Barbecue Pizza Unroll a ready-rolled sheet of shortcrust pastry and place on a baking sheet. Spread 4 tablespoons pizza topping sauce over the top. Chop 250 g (8 oz) cooked chicken, mix with 2 tablespoons smoky barbecue sauce and scatter over the top. Chop 125 g (4 oz) roasted red peppers from a jar, slice 150 g (5 oz) mozzarella cheese and arrange on top. Bake in a preheated oven, 200°C (400°F), Gas Mark 6, for 15 minutes or until crisp and golden.

1 Cheesy Chicken Omelette

Serves 2

4 eggs
15 g (½ oz) butter
75 g (3 oz) cooked chicken,
  chopped
50 g (2 oz) Gruyère cheese,
  grated
salt and pepper
salad, to serve

- Put a small nonstick frying pan on the hob to heat. Crack the eggs into a bowl, season with salt and pepper and add 1 tablespoon cold water. Beat with a fork until evenly mixed.

- Add the butter to the pan. When it is foaming and melted pour in the beaten egg mixture. As the eggs begin to set, use a wooden spoon to draw the mixture into the centre of the pan, allowing the runny egg to flow to the edge of the pan.

- When the top of the omelette is softly set arrange the chicken and cheese down the centre. Starting at the side nearest the handle, flip the omelette over the filling and then tip it out on to a plate. Cut in half and serve with a simple salad.

 2 Frittata

Beat together 4 eggs and season with salt and pepper. Heat 1 tablespoon olive oil in a small frying pan with a heatproof handle. Add 200 g (7 oz) chopped cooked potatoes and fry for 5 minutes until golden. Add 2 chopped spring onions, 75 g (3 oz) chopped cooked chicken and a handful of frozen peas. Heat through, then pour over the eggs. Cook until just set. Arrange 50 g (2 oz) sliced Gruyère on top and grill until the frittata is just firm and the cheese has melted.

 3 Soufflé Omelette

Separate 4 eggs. Season the egg yolks and whisk the egg whites until they form soft peaks. Lightly fold the egg whites into the egg yolks. Melt 15 g (½ oz) butter in a large frying pan. When it is foaming add the egg mixture and spread it out evenly. When it is set arrange 75 g (3 oz) chopped cooked chicken and 50 g (2 oz) sliced Gruyère cheese over the top. Place the pan under a medium grill until the egg is set and the cheese has melted. Fold over the omelette and slide out on to a plate. Serve with tomato salad.

3 Chicken Quesadillas with Coriander and Chilli

Serves 4

8 soft flour tortillas
220 g (7½ oz) can refried beans
250 g (8 oz) cooked chicken, chopped
1 red chilli, deseeded and finely chopped
4 tomatoes, finely chopped
handful of fresh coriander leaves, roughly chopped
175 g (6 oz) mature Cheddar cheese, grated
3 tablespoons olive oil
lettuce and sweetcorn salad, to serve

- Spread 4 of the tortillas with the refried beans, top with the cooked chicken, chopped chilli, tomatoes, coriander and grated cheese. Cover with the remaining tortillas, pressing them together firmly.

- Heat 1 tablespoon olive oil in a large frying pan, add one quesadilla and fry for 3 minutes on each side until the cheese has melted and the quesadilla is golden and crisp. Remove from the pan and keep warm. Repeat with the remaining quesadillas, adding a little more oil as necessary.

- Cut into wedges and serve warm with crisp lettuce and sweetcorn salad.

---

1 Chilli Chicken Nachos

Spread 150 g (5 oz) tortilla chips in the bottom of a large ovenproof dish. Dot with 220 g (7½ oz) can refried beans, 175 g (6 oz) chopped cooked chicken and 4 tablespoons spicy tomato salsa. Sprinkle over 125 g (4 oz) grated Cheddar cheese and place under a medium grill until the cheese has melted. Sprinkle with chopped fresh coriander and serve.

2 Chicken and Chilli Wraps

Spread 4 tomato-flavoured soft flour tortilla wraps with 220 g (7½ oz) can refried beans. Chop 250 g (8 oz) cooked chicken and place evenly down the centre of each tortilla. Top with 1 chopped red chilli, 3 chopped tomatoes and a handful of roughly chopped fresh coriander leaves. Sprinkle 175 g (6 oz) grated Cheddar cheese on the top and roll up.

Cut each wrap in half and arrange in an ovenproof dish. Sprinkle with a little extra cheese and bake in a preheated oven, 200°C (400°F), Gas Mark 6, for 10 minutes or until golden and crisp.

Spiced Chicken Naans

Serves 2

4 tablespoons natural yogurt
1 tablespoon jalfrezi curry paste
2 tablespoons lemon juice
2 skinless chicken breast fillets,
 each cut into 8 pieces
1 small red onion, thinly sliced
1 small green pepper, cored,
 deseeded and thinly sliced
4 tablespoons passata
2 garlic and coriander naan breads
150 g (5 oz) mozzarella cheese,
 drained and sliced

- Mix together the yogurt, jalfrezi paste and lemon juice. Add the chicken pieces and stir to coat. Place the chicken on a foil-lined grill pan with the onion and pepper slices and cook under a preheated hot grill for 5–8 minutes, turning occasionally, until the chicken is cooked and beginning to char at the edges and the onion and pepper slices have softened slightly.

- Spread the passata over the naan breads, top with the chicken, onion, pepper and mozzarella. Line the grill pan with a clean piece of foil. Place the naan breads on the foil, reduce the grill to medium heat and cook the naan 'pizzas' for 5–8 minutes or until the cheese has melted and the topping is hot.

 Spiced Chicken Salad with Poppadoms Mix together 4 tablespoons mayonnaise with 1 teaspoon mild curry paste, 2 tablespoons mango chutney and 1 tablespoon roughly chopped fresh coriander leaves. Stir in 200 g (7 oz) ready-cooked chicken tikka and half a chopped apple. Serve with chopped cucumber and ready-to-eat poppadoms.

 Hot Spiced Chicken and Mango Chutney Chapati Wraps Mix 2 chopped skinless chicken breast fillets with 4 tablespoons natural yogurt, 1 tablespoon jalfrezi paste and 2 tablespoons lemon juice. Cook under a hot grill for 5–8 minutes, turning occasionally, until cooked and beginning to char at the edges. Place on 2 warmed chapatis with 1 small, thinly sliced red onion, fresh coriander leaves and 2 tablespoons mango chutney. Roll up the chapatis and serve warm.

20 Mozzarella Chicken Melts

Serves 4

1 tablespoon sun-dried tomato pesto

2 tablespoons olive oil

2 chicken breasts, halved horizontally

4 thick slices of sourdough bread

2 tablespoons tapenade

175 g (6 oz) cherry tomatoes, halved

small handful of basil leaves, roughly torn

150 g (5 oz) mozzarella cheese, drained and sliced

green salad, to serve

- Mix together the tomato pesto and 1 tablespoon olive oil and spread over both sides of the chicken pieces.

- Heat the remaining olive oil in a frying pan, add the chicken and cook for 8–10 minutes, turning once until the chicken is cooked through.

- Toast both sides of the sourdough bread, spread one side with the tapenade, top with the cooked chicken, cherry tomatoes, basil and mozzarella. Cook under a preheated grill until the tomatoes are hot and the mozzarella has melted. Serve with a simple green salad.

10 Italian Chicken Toasties

Butter 8 slices of crusty bread. Spread the unbuttered side of 4 slices with 2 tablespoons tapenade. Top with 200 g (7 oz) sliced cooked chicken, 2 sliced tomatoes, a handful of basil leaves and 150 g (5 oz) sliced mozzarella cheese. Top with the remaining bread, butter side up. Cook in a sandwich toaster for about 5 minutes until golden and crisp or in a frying pan, turning once, until the bread is crisp and the filling is hot.

30 Baked Chicken

Coat 2 halved chicken breasts in a mixture of 1 tablespoon sun-dried tomato paste and 1 tablespoon olive oil. Season and place in a baking dish with 175 g (6 oz) halved cherry tomatoes, 1 thinly sliced courgette and a small handful of torn basil leaves. Arrange 150 g (5 oz) sliced mozzarella on top and drizzle with a little olive oil. Cook in a preheated oven, 200°C (400°F), Gas Mark 6, for 25 minutes until the chicken is cooked and the vegetables are tender. Serve with crusty bread.

 # Smoked Chicken Bruschetta

Serves 4

½ ciabatta loaf, cut into 1 cm
   (½ inch) slices
2 tablespoons olive oil
1 garlic clove, crushed
2 spring onions, finely chopped
4 ripe tomatoes, finely chopped
1 tablespoon chopped basil
1 tablespoon balsamic vinegar
1 smoked cooked chicken breast,
   torn into small pieces
salt and pepper

- Place the bread slices on a baking sheet. Mix together the oil and garlic and brush over the bread. Bake in a preheated oven, 180°C (350°F), Gas Mark 4, for 10 minutes until crisp.

- Meanwhile, mix together the spring onions, tomatoes, basil and balsamic vinegar. Season with salt and pepper, then toss in the chicken pieces.

- Spoon the tomato mixture on to the toasts to serve.

 ### Smoked Chicken Ciabatta

Combine the tomato and spring onion as above and spread over ready-made ciabatta toasts. Top with sliced smoked chicken and basil leaves.

 ### Smoked Chicken and Tomato Tarts

Cut a sheet of ready-rolled puff pastry into 4 rectangles. Use a sharp knife to score a line 1 cm (½ inch) in around the edges. Transfer to a baking sheet, lightly brush with beaten egg and bake in a preheated oven, 200°C (400°F), Gas Mark 6, for 15 minutes or until well risen and golden. Push the centre section down with your fingers and spoon in a mixture of 2 finely chopped spring onions, 4 chopped tomatoes, 1 tablespoon chopped basil and 1 tablespoon balsamic vinegar, seasoned with salt and pepper. Top with slices of smoked chicken and garnish with basil leaves.

Lemon, Mint and Chicken Skewers

Serves 4

150 g (5 oz) Greek yogurt
finely grated rind and juice of
  1 lemon
2 tablespoons chopped mint
2 tablespoons olive oil
4 skinless chicken breast fillets,
  each cut into 8 pieces
salt and pepper

To serve

pitta breads, warmed
cucumber, sliced
radish, sliced

• Mix together the yogurt, lemon rind and juice, mint and olive oil. Add the chicken pieces and stir well to coat.

• Thread the chicken on to 4 skewers and place on a foil-lined grill pan. Cook under a preheated hot grill for about 10 minutes, turning occasionally, or until the chicken is cooked and slightly charred at the edges. Slide the chicken off the skewers and serve in warm pitta breads with slices of cucumber and radish.

 Lemon Chicken Pittas

Make a lemon mint dressing by mixing together 2 tablespoons mayonnaise, 2 tablespoons Greek yogurt, 1 teaspoon finely grated lemon rind and 1 tablespoon chopped mint. Warm 4 pitta breads and top with sliced cooked chicken, sliced cucumber and sliced radish. Top with the lemon mint dressing.

 Baked Lemon Chicken with Garlic Roast Tomatoes

Coat 4 skinless chicken breast fillets, each cut in half widthways, in a mixture of 150 ml (¼ pint) Greek yogurt, the finely grated rind and juice of 1 lemon, 2 tablespoons chopped mint and 2 tablespoons olive oil. Place on a foil-lined baking sheet with 4 halved tomatoes sprinkled with 1 chopped garlic clove, olive oil and salt and pepper. Bake in a preheated oven, 220°C (425°F), Gas Mark 7, for 20 minutes, turning once, until the chicken is cooked and the tomatoes are soft. Serve with oven chips.

QuickCook
Midweek Meals

Recipes listed by cooking time

30

20

20 Chicken Pesto Pasta

Serves 4

375 g (12 oz) penne or other
  pasta shapes
large handful of basil leaves
25 g (1 oz) toasted pine nuts,
  plus extra to serve
25 g (1 oz) freshly grated
  Parmesan cheese, plus extra
  to serve
1 garlic clove, peeled
3 tablespoons olive oil
175 g (6 oz) cooked chicken
handful of chopped black olives
salt and pepper

• Cook the penne in lightly salted boiling water for 10 minutes or until just tender.

• Meanwhile, make the pesto. Put the basil, pine nuts, Parmesan, garlic and olive oil in a small food processor or blender and process until almost smooth.

• Drain the cooked penne and return to the pan. Add the pesto, chicken and olives. Season with salt and pepper and gently heat through. Serve sprinkled with extra pine nuts and Parmesan.

 10 Chicken Pasta Salad with Pesto Dressing Cook 250 g (8 oz) quick-cook pasta bows in lightly salted boiling water for 5 minutes or until just tender. Drain, rinse under running cold water and drain again. Mix with 1 tablespoon ready-made pesto, 1 tablespoon olive oil and 1 teaspoon balsamic vinegar. Add 200 g (7 oz) cooked chopped chicken, 8 halved cherry tomatoes, 50 g (2 oz) baby spinach leaves and a handful of toasted pine nuts. Lightly mix together and serve.

 30 Crispy Pesto Breadcrumbed Chicken Cut 4 skinless chicken breast fillets in half horizontally and put them on a foil-lined baking sheet. Spread each piece of chicken with 1 teaspoon ready-made pesto and cover with 100 g (3½ oz) ready-made lemon and black pepper flavoured breadcrumbs. Drizzle generously with olive oil and bake in a preheated oven, 200°C (400°F), Gas Mark 6, for 25 minutes or until the chicken is cooked and the breadcrumbs are crisp. Serve with oven chips and broccoli.

30 Moroccan Fruity Chicken Stew

Serves 4

1 tablespoon olive oil
1 large red onion, cut in large
  chunks
1 onion, cut into large chunks
375 g (12 oz) diced chicken
1 teaspoon ground cumin
1 teaspoon paprika
1 teaspoon ground coriander
½ teaspoon ground cinnamon
½ teaspoon ground ginger
125 g (4 oz) dried prunes
125 g (4 oz) dried apricots
400 g (13 oz) can chickpeas
600 ml (1 pint) rich chicken stock
1 tablespoon cornflour, blended
  with 2 tablespoons water
4 tablespoons chopped coriander

- Heat the oil in a large, heavy-based saucepan and cook the onions and chicken, stirring occasionally, over a moderately high heat for 10 minutes or until golden in places and soft. Add the spices, stir and cook for a further 2 minutes to help the flavours infuse.

- Add the prunes and apricots, chickpeas and stock and bring to the boil. Cover and cook for 15 minutes until all the ingredients are soft and cooked through.

- Add the blended cornflour and stir well to thicken slightly, then stir in the fresh coriander. Serve with couscous, if liked.

---

1 Moroccan Chicken and Bean Soup

Heat 1 tablespoon olive oil in a saucepan and cook 1 thinly sliced red onion and 250 g (8 oz) thinly sliced chicken breast for 3–4 minutes. Add 1 teaspoon ground cumin, 1 teaspoon ground coriander and ½ teaspoon ground cinnamon and cook for 30 seconds. Pour in 600 ml (1 pint) chicken stock and 400 g (13 oz) can drained chickpeas. Boil, reduce the heat and add 50 g (2 oz) roughly chopped dried prunes. Cook for 4 minutes more until piping hot. Process in a blender for a smooth soup, if liked.

2 Moroccan Jacket Potatoes

Cook 4 baking potatoes in the microwave oven for about 15 minutes. Meanwhile, heat 1 tablespoon olive oil in a large, heavy-based saucepan and cook 1 sliced onion with 2 thinly sliced chicken breasts, each about 150 g (5 oz), over a high heat for 5 minutes. Add ½ teaspoon each of ground cumin, ground coriander, ground paprika and ground cinnamon and cook for a further 1 minute. Chop 175 g (6 oz) mixed ready-to-eat dried prunes and apricots, add to the pan with 150 ml (¼ pint) chicken stock and bring to the boil. Reduce the heat and simmer gently for 5 minutes. Add 400 g (13 oz) can mixed beans in tomato sauce and heat for a further 3–4 minutes, stirring occasionally, until piping hot and the chicken is thoroughly cooked. Serve the sauce spooned into the cooked potatoes.

30 Warm Chicken Liver, Butternut Squash and Bacon Salad

Serves 4

4 tablespoons olive oil
750 g (1½ lb) butternut squash, deseeded and cut into small chunks (peeled if liked)
380 g (12½ oz) chicken livers, thawed if frozen and drained
175 g (6 oz) streaky bacon, cut into strips
100 g (3½ oz) walnuts
160 g (5½ oz) watercress
pepper
balsamic vinegar, to serve

- Heat 3 tablespoons of the oil in a large, heavy-based frying pan or wok and cook the butternut squash, stirring occasionally, over a moderately high heat for 15–20 minutes until softened and cooked through.

- Meanwhile, in a separate heavy-based frying pan heat the remaining oil and cook the chicken livers and bacon, stirring almost continually to prevent sticking, over a high heat for 10 minutes or until golden and cooked through. Add the walnuts and cook for a further minute to warm through.

- Toss together the chicken livers, bacon, walnuts and butternut squash in a large bowl, season with pepper and set aside to cool for 3–4 minutes.

- Just before serving toss the watercress into the bowl. Arrange the salad on 4 warmed serving plates and drizzle with balsamic vinegar.

 Chicken Liver, Bacon and Pine Nut Salad Heat 2 tablespoons olive oil in a large, heavy-based frying pan and cook 250 g (8 oz) drained chicken livers together with 175 g (6 oz) chopped streaky bacon over a high heat for 5 minutes. Meanwhile, put 3 tablespoons pine nuts into a small pan and cook over a gentle heat for 3–4 minutes until lightly toasted. Place 150 g (5 oz) watercress in a large salad bowl and toss with the warm chicken livers and bacon and toasted pine nuts. Dress with balsamic vinegar and olive oil.

 Chicken Liver and Bacon Salad with Peppers and Onions Core and deseed 1 red and 1 orange pepper and cut into chunks. Heat 2 tablespoons olive oil in a large, heavy-based frying pan and cook the pepper with 1 thinly sliced red onion for 4–5 minutes until softened and golden in places. Remove from the pan with a slotted spoon, then add 250 g (8 oz) drained chicken livers and 175 g (6 oz) chopped streaky bacon and cook over a high heat for 4 minutes until cooked through. Add 100 g (3½ oz) walnuts and cook for a further 2 minutes. Transfer to a large bowl with 150 g (5 oz) baby spinach leaves and toss well. Drizzle with balsamic vinegar to serve.

Coronation Chicken

Serves 4

150 ml (¼ pint) mayonnaise
1–2 teaspoons medium curry paste
1 tablespoon lemon juice
1 tablespoon chopped fresh coriander
375 g (12 oz) cooked chicken, chopped
125 g (4 oz) seedless grapes, halved
2 tablespoons raisins
salt and pepper

To serve
watercress
crusty bread

- Mix together the mayonnaise, curry paste, lemon juice and half the coriander. Season with salt and pepper.

- Lightly stir in the chicken, grapes and raisins. Sprinkle with the remaining coriander and serve with watercress and crusty bread.

---

2 **Coronation Chicken and Three Grains Salad** Cook 125 g (4 oz) three grains risotto mix (rice, barley and spelt) in lightly salted boiling water for 10 minutes or until just tender. Drain, rinse under running cold water and drain again. Lightly stir into the coronation chicken mixture and sprinkle with toasted flaked almonds.

3 **Coronation Chicken and Potato Salad** Cook 400 g (13 oz) new potatoes in lightly salted boiling water for 10–15 minutes or until tender. Drain and cut in half. Leave to cool, then mix with 375 g (12 oz) chopped cooked chicken, 150 ml (¼ pint) mayonnaise, 1–2 teaspoons medium curry paste, 1 tablespoon lemon juice, 1 tablespoon chopped fresh coriander and a small bunch of spring onions, chopped.

Pan-Fried Chicken with Garlicky Bean Mash

Serves 4

8 small boneless, skinless chicken thighs
1 tablespoon sunflower oil
1 tablespoon wholegrain mustard
150 ml (¼ pint) apple juice
   or dry cider
2 × 400 g (13 oz) cans butter beans, rinsed and drained
4 tablespoons garlic-flavoured oil
2 tablespoons roughly chopped flat leaf parsley
salt and pepper

- Flatten the chicken thighs and season well with salt and pepper. Heat the oil in a frying pan, add the chicken thighs and cook over a high heat for 5 minutes, turning once, until golden.

- Stir the mustard and apple juice or cider into the pan, reduce the heat and simmer for 10 minutes or until the sauce is reduced and slightly thickened.

- Meanwhile, heat the butter beans in a pan with the garlic oil and 2 tablespoons water for a few minutes until hot. Mash with a potato masher, season with salt and pepper and stir in the flat leaf parsley. Serve with the chicken and the pan juices.

10 **Mustard Chicken with Kale and Butter Beans** Fry 400 g (13 oz) mini-chicken fillets in 1 tablespoon sunflower oil for 3 minutes. Stir in 1 tablespoon wholegrain mustard, 200 g (7 oz) washed curly kale and 400 g (13 oz) can butter beans, rinsed and drained. Cover and cook for 5 minutes until the kale is tender. Stir in 200 ml (7 fl oz) crème fraîche, season, heat through and serve.

30 **Stuffed Chicken Thighs with Bean Mash** Flatten 8 small boneless, skinless chicken thighs. Spread them with 175 g (6 oz) soft blue cheese, roll up, wrap in 8 slices of streaky bacon and secure each with cocktail sticks. Fry in 1 tablespoon sunflower oil over a high heat for 5 minutes, turning occasionally, until browned. Add 1 tablespoon wholegrain mustard and 150 ml (¼ pint) apple juice or dry cider and simmer for 10–15 minutes or until the chicken is cooked through. Serve with butter bean mash as above.

30 Chicken and Piquante Pepper Tortilla

Serves 4

2 tablespoons olive oil

1 large red onion, sliced

250 g (8 oz) chicken thigh meat, thinly sliced

5 tablespoons chopped parsley

1 tablespoon chopped rosemary leaves

375 g (12 oz) jar piquante peppers, drained

5 eggs, beaten

salt and pepper

· Heat the oil in a large, heavy-based frying pan, about 25 cm (10 inches) across, and cook the onion and chicken for 8–10 minutes over a moderately high heat or until soft and cooked through. Add the parsley, rosemary and peppers and stir and cook for a further 2 minutes.

· Beat the eggs in a jug with plenty of salt and pepper. Pour over the chicken and onions and cook gently over a low heat for 5 minutes until the base is set. Place under a preheated hot grill to cook the top for 4–5 minutes until just set. Serve cut into wedges with a simple salad and crusty bread, if liked.

 1 Fluffy Chicken and Pepper Wok Omelette Finely chop 1 small red onion. Heat 2 tablespoons olive oil in a large wok and cook the onion for 3 minutes. Add 100 g (3½ oz) diced cooked chicken and 50 g (2 oz) roughly chopped and drained, piquante peppers and 2 tablespoons chopped frozen parsley. Pour in 6 beaten eggs and cook over a high heat until the base is beginning to set. Keep flipping the omelette in the pan until both sides are just set. Sprinkle with some freshly grated Parmesan cheese, if liked, and serve cut into 4 pieces.

 2 Chicken and Piquante Pepper Omelette Heat 1 tablespoon olive oil in a large, heavy-based frying pan and cook 1 large sliced red onion and 250 g (8 oz) chopped chicken thigh meat over a moderately high heat, stirring occasionally, for 8–10 minutes or until golden and cooked. Drain 300 g (10 oz) jar piquante peppers and add to the pan with 1 tablespoon chopped rosemary. Season generously and cook for a further 1 minute to heat through. Heat a further 1 tablespoon olive oil in a 20 cm (8 inch) heavy-based frying pan and cook half the egg mixture as above in the pan over a gentle heat for 3–4 minutes. Remove from the pan with a fish slice and keep warm while heating a further 1 tablespoon olive oil and cooking the remaining egg to make a second thin omelette. Fill each with half the chicken mixture, flip over the omelette to enclose and cut each in half to serve.

Chicken, Chorizo and Broccoli Pasta

Serves 4

250 g (8 oz) rigatoni or other
  pasta shapes
125 g (4 oz) broccoli florets
2 tablespoons olive oil
2 skinless chicken breast fillets,
  sliced
175 g (6 oz) chorizo, thickly sliced
200 ml (7 fl oz) crème fraîche
4 teaspoons chopped parsley
salt and pepper
freshly grated Parmesan cheese,
  to serve

- Cook the rigatoni in lightly salted boiling water for 10 minutes or until just tender, adding the broccoli for the final 5 minutes of the cooking time.

- Meanwhile, heat the oil in a frying pan, add the chicken and chorizo and fry for 5–8 minutes or until the chicken is cooked through. Stir in the crème fraîche and heat through, then add the parsley. Add a little water if the sauce becomes too thick.

- Add the pasta and broccoli and stir well to mix. Season with salt and pepper and serve with plenty of freshly grated Parmesan cheese.

 Chicken and Tomato Ravioli

Cook 350 g (11½ oz) ready-made chilled spinach- and ricotta-filled ravioli in lightly salted boiling water for 3 minutes or according to the instructions on the packet. Drain, tip back into the pan, add 175 g (6 oz) chopped cooked chicken, 75 g (3 oz) chopped cooked chorizo and 350 g (11½ oz) ready-made tomato and basil sauce. Heat through and serve with freshly grated Parmesan cheese.

Chicken, Chorizo and Leek Lasagne

Fry 2 chopped skinless chicken breast fillets, 175 g (6 oz) chopped chorizo and 1 sliced leek in 2 tablespoons olive oil over a high heat for 5 minutes. Stir in 350 g (11½ oz) ready-made tomato pasta sauce and heat through. Layer sheets of fresh lasagne and the tomato mixture in an ovenproof dish. Pour 350 g (11½ oz) ready-made fresh cheese sauce over the top and bake in a preheated oven, 200°C (400°F), Gas Mark 6, for 20 minutes until golden and bubbling. Serve with broccoli.

CHI-MIDW-TAR

30 Thai Red Curry with Chicken Meatballs

Serves 4

500 g (1 lb) chicken mince
1 tablespoon lemon grass paste
1 teaspoon minced ginger paste
7 tablespoons chopped fresh
  coriander
1 small red bird's eye chilli, finely
  chopped
1 tablespoon vegetable oil
2 tablespoon red Thai curry paste
400 ml (14 fl oz) can coconut milk
salt and pepper
boiled rice, to serve (optional)

- Put the mince in a large bowl with the lemon grass paste, ginger paste, 3 tablespoons of the chopped fresh coriander and the chopped red chilli. Season well with a little salt and pepper and mix well with a fork to blend the spices into the chicken. Shape the mixture into 32 walnut-sized balls.

- Heat the oil in a large, heavy-based frying pan and cook the meatballs over a high heat for 8–10 minutes, in batches if necessary, until golden in places, lightly shaking the pan to turn the meatballs. Mix the curry paste into the coconut milk and pour over the meatballs. Bring to the boil, reduce the heat and simmer for 5 minutes. Stir in the remaining fresh coriander and serve with boiled rice, if liked.

---

1 **Thai Burgers**
Put 375 g (12 oz) minced chicken in a bowl with 1 tablespoon Thai curry paste and 3 tablespoons chopped fresh coriander. Shape the flavoured mince into 4 patty shapes and flatten as much as possible without the patties breaking. Heat 1 tablespoon vegetable oil in a large, heavy-based frying pan and cook the patties for 2–3 minutes on each side over a high heat until golden and cooked. Serve in buns with salad.

2 **Thai Chicken Stir-Fry**
Prepare 500 g (1 lb) chicken mince as above, blending it with the lemon grass, ginger, fresh coriander and chilli. Heat 1 tablespoon vegetable oil in a large wok or frying pan and cook the mince, stirring occasionally, over a high heat for 7–8 minutes until the mince is golden and crispy in places. Add 300 g (10 oz) sugar snap peas, 1 chopped red pepper and 1 chopped orange pepper.

Stir-fry for a further 4 minutes, add 200 ml (7 fl oz) coconut milk and 2 teaspoons red Thai curry paste and cook, stirring, for 2 minutes until piping hot. Serve spooned into warmed serving bowls.

1 Chicken Satay

Serves 4

12 ready-made chicken satay skewers

2 × 250 g (8 oz) packets ready-cooked Thai rice

4 tablespoons mayonnaise

2 tablespoons crunchy peanut butter

1 teaspoon Thai red curry paste

2 spring onions, sliced

- Reheat the chicken satay skewers in a microwave oven or in a hot frying pan for 2–3 minutes.

- Reheat the rice in a microwave oven or saucepan according to the instructions on the packets.

- Mix together the mayonnaise, peanut butter and Thai curry paste and pour into a small serving bowl.

- Serve the chicken skewers with the rice and sauce, with the spring onions sprinkled over.

---

2 Chicken Satay and Noodle Salad

Soak 200 g (7 oz) rice vermicelli noodles in boiling water for a few minutes until softened, then drain. Meanwhile, stir-fry 3 sliced skinless chicken breast fillets in 1 tablespoon groundnut oil for 5 minutes. Add 1 tablespoon dark soy sauce and 1 tablespoon sweet chilli sauce and simmer for 1 minute. Mix together the noodles and chicken with 125 g (4 oz) baby spinach leaves and 125 g (4 oz) mangetout. Pour over a dressing of 2 tablespoons crunchy peanut butter, 1 tablespoon sweet chilli sauce, 2 tablespoons lemon juice and 1 tablespoon groundnut oil.

3 Chicken Satay Skewers

Cut 4 skinless chicken breast fillets into strips and coat in a mixture of 1 tablespoon dark soy sauce, 1 teaspoon dark brown sugar, 1 teaspoon lemon grass paste and 1 teaspoon Thai red curry paste. Leave to marinate for 10 minutes. Thread the chicken on to skewers, concertina style, and place them on a foil-lined grill pan. Cook under a preheated hot grill for 5 minutes until cooked through. Make a peanut dipping sauce. Warm 2 tablespoons crunchy peanut butter with 1 teaspoon Thai red curry paste and 4 tablespoons coconut cream.

Serve the chicken skewers with the peanut sauce separately and a crisp salad.

Basil, Ricotta and Sun-Dried Tomato Chicken

Serves 4

4 chicken breast fillet, skin on
200 g (7 oz) ricotta cheese
small handful of basil leaves
125 g (4 oz) sun-dried tomatoes
2 tablespoons olive oil
salt and pepper

To serve

spinach
new potatoes

- Cut a slit along the length of each chicken breast to make a large pocket. Spread the ricotta in the pockets and top with basil leaves and sun-dried tomatoes. Press the chicken together firmly to close the pockets. Season the chicken with salt and pepper.

- Heat the oil in a large frying pan, add the chicken breasts, skin side down, and fry for 15 minutes, turning once, until golden and the chicken is cooked through. Serve with spinach and new potatoes and the juices from the pan.

Mediterranean Omelette (serves 2)

Beat together 6 eggs with 2 tablespoons water. Season with salt and pepper. Heat 25 g (1 oz) butter in a large frying pan until foaming, pour in the beaten eggs and cook for 1 minute. Use a wooden spatula to draw the set egg into the centre of the pan allowing the uncooked egg to run to the sides. When golden brown underneath and softly set on top dot with 125 g (4 oz) ricotta cheese, a few basil leaves, 125 g (4 oz) thinly sliced cooked chicken and 125 g (4 oz) chopped sun-dried tomatoes. Fold the omelette in half and slide on to a serving plate to serve.

Baked Basil and Ricotta Chicken with Roasted Vegetables

Cut 4 chicken breasts (with skin on) down the side to form pockets. Fill with 200 g (7 oz) ricotta cheese, a few basil leaves and 125 g (4 oz) chopped sun-dried tomatoes. Press together firmly and place on baking sheet with 2 sliced courgettes, 1 cored and deseeded red pepper, 3 unpeeled garlic cloves and 375 g (12 oz) new potatoes (halved if large). Season, drizzle with olive oil and add a few sprigs of rosemary. Roast in a preheated oven, 200°C (400°F), Gas Mark 6, for 25 minutes until the chicken is cooked and the vegetables are tender.

30 Chicken, Feta and Spinach Pasties

Serves 4

175 g (6 oz) frozen leaf spinach, thawed and well drained
175 g (6 oz) cooked chicken breast, torn into pieces
½ teaspoon ground nutmeg
25 g (1 oz) softened butter
3 tablespoons toasted pine nuts
50 g (2 oz) feta cheese, crumbled
8 sheets of filo pastry
salt and pepper
salad, to serve

- Put the spinach in a bowl with the chicken, nutmeg and half the softened butter and mix together. Season with plenty of pepper and a little salt. Add the pine nuts and feta and mix to combine.

- Place the sheets of filo pastry on a board and fold in half widthways. Spoon the chicken mixture evenly on to each piece and fold one side over to cover the filling. Fold the other side over, then fold the opposite sides, one under and one over the filling, to form a square. Place on a baking sheet. Melt the remaining butter and brush each pasty lightly.

- Bake in a preheated oven, 200°C (400°F), Gas Mark 6, for 15 minutes until golden and cooked through. Serve with a simple salad.

10 Chicken, Feta and Spinach Stir-Fry

Heat 2 tablespoons oil in a large wok or frying pan and cook 2 thinly sliced chicken breast fillets for 5 minutes. Add 300 g (10 oz) ready-prepared spinach leaves and ½ teaspoon grated nutmeg, toss and stir for 2 minutes until wilted. Season generously with salt and pepper and scatter over 200 g (7 oz) crumbled feta cheese and 3 tablespoons toasted pine nuts. Serve with plenty of crusty bread.

20 Chicken and Spinach Tarts

Cut 4 sheets of filo pastry in half. Fold each piece in half widthways and place in a 4-portion Yorkshire pudding tin, ruffling the pastry so that it fits the tin. Lightly brush with 15 g (½ oz) melted butter and bake in a preheated oven, 200°C (400°F), Gas Mark 6, for 5–6 minutes until golden and crisp. Meanwhile, put 15 g (½ oz) butter in a pan and add 250 g (8 oz) torn cooked chicken

breast, 250 g (8 oz) thawed leaf spinach and ½ teaspoon nutmeg. Heat, stirring, for 5 minutes until piping hot. Stir in 3 tablespoons toasted pine nuts and 50 g (2 oz) crumbled feta cheese and remove from the heat. Spoon the hot filling into the 4 hot pastry cases and serve with a simple salad.

 # Thai Red Curry Soup

Serves 4

1 tablespoon sunflower oil
2 skinless chicken breast fillets,
    cut into strips
375 g (12 oz) butternut squash,
    peeled and cut into small pieces
1 red pepper, cored, deseeded
    and cut into small pieces
1 tablespoon Thai red curry paste
400 ml (14 fl oz) can reduced-fat
    coconut milk
600 ml (1 pint) chicken stock
175 g (6 oz) green beans, halved
small handful of fresh coriander
    leaves, roughly chopped

· Heat the oil in a large saucepan, add the chicken,
  butternut squash and red pepper and fry over a high
  heat for 5 minutes.

· Add the curry paste, fry for 1 minute then stir in the
  coconut milk, stock and green beans. Bring to the boil,
  reduce the heat, cover and simmer for 10 minutes until
  the chicken and vegetables are cooked. Stir in the fresh
  coriander and serve.

---

10 Chicken, Butternut Squash and Vermicelli Soup Heat 600 g (1 pint) ready-made chilled spiced butternut squash soup in a saucepan. Stir in 125 g (4 oz) chopped cooked chicken and 75 g (3 oz) vermicelli rice noodles. Simmer for 5 minutes until the noodles are soft.

30 Spiced Thai Chicken and Rice Fry 8 small chicken thighs (with skin on) in 1 tablespoon vegetable oil over a high heat for 5 minutes, turning once. Add 375 g (12 oz) finely chopped butternut squash, 1 finely chopped red pepper and 125 g (4 oz) halved green beans and cook for a further 5 minutes. Stir in 1 tablespoon Thai red curry paste, 250 g (8 oz) long grain rice, 400 ml (14 fl oz) can coconut milk and 450 ml (¾ pint) chicken stock. Simmer for 15–20 minutes until the liquid is absorbed and the rice is tender. Scatter over fresh coriander leaves to serve.

30 Potato, Chicken, Bacon and Thyme Gratin

Serves 4

500 g (1 lb) potatoes (not peeled), thinly sliced
2 tablespoons olive oil
1 onion, thinly sliced
2 chicken breasts, each about 150 g (5 oz), thinly sliced
6 back bacon rashers, thinly sliced
3 tablespoons thyme leaves
300 ml (½ pint) double cream
5 tablespoons freshly grated Parmesan cheese
salt and pepper

- Cook the potatoes in a large saucepan of lightly salted boiling water for 10 minutes until just tender, then drain.

- Meanwhile, heat the oil in a large, heavy-based frying pan and cook the onion, chicken and bacon over a high heat, stirring occasionally, for 5 minutes or until cooked through.

- Layer the potatoes in a large, shallow gratin dish with the chicken, bacon, onion and a scattering of thyme leaves, ending with a layer of potatoes. Season the cream with a little salt and pepper and pour over the potatoes. Scatter over the Parmesan and cook under a preheated hot grill for 4–5 minutes until the topping is golden and the cream bubbling. Serve with a simple green salad.

---

1 Chicken, Bacon and Thyme Stir-Fry

Heat 2 tablespoons olive oil in a large, heavy-based frying pan and cook 3 thinly sliced chicken breasts, each about 150 g (5 oz), and 175 g (6 oz) chopped bacon pieces for 8 minutes, stirring occasionally, then add 1 tablespoon thyme leaves and 400 ml (14 fl oz) crème fraîche. Season generously and serve with instant mashed potato with freshly grated Parmesan cheese sprinkled over.

2 Creamy Chicken and Bacon Pie

Slice 2 potatoes and cook in a large saucepan of lightly salted boiling water for 10 minutes or until tender, then drain. Meanwhile, heat 1 tablespoon oil in a large, heavy-based wok or frying pan and cook 350 g (12 oz) diced chicken and 175 g (6 oz) chopped bacon for 10 minutes until golden. Add 1 tablespoon thyme leaves and 2 × 300 ml (½ pint) cans condensed chicken soup and heat for 2–3 minutes until hot. Transfer to a large, shallow gratin dish and top with the drained potato slices. Lightly brush the top with 1 tablespoon olive oil and scatter with 3 tablespoons freshly grated Parmesan cheese. Cook under a hot grill for 2–3 minutes until golden.

3⦿ Crispy Salt and Pepper Chicken Thighs

Serves 4

8 chicken thighs, each about
125 g (4 oz)
50 g (2 oz) plain flour
½ teaspoon salt flakes
1 teaspoon black pepper
1 tablespoon olive oil
3 teaspoons thyme leaves,
to garnish

- Tighten the flesh and skin around the bone of each chicken thigh and pierce with a cocktail skewer so that the skin remains taut.

- Put the flour in a large bowl with half the salt and pepper and toss the thighs in the seasoned flour until lightly coated.

- Heat the oil in a large, heavy-based frying pan and cook the chicken, skin side up, for 5 minutes, turning once, until golden.

- Transfer the chicken to a roasting tin, skin side up, and scatter over the remaining salt and pepper. Cook in a preheated oven, 200°C (400°F), Gas Mark 6, for 20–25 minutes until the chicken is golden and cooked through; when the chicken is pierced the juices should run clear.

- Scatter over the thyme leaves to garnish and serve with simple green vegetables or a crisp salad.

 1 Salt and Pepper Mini-Breast Fillets
Put 50 g (2 oz) plain flour in a bowl and season with 1 teaspoon black pepper and a little salt. Toss 500 g (1 lb) mini-chicken fillets in the seasoned flour until lightly coated. Heat 4 tablespoons olive oil in a large, heavy-based frying pan or wok and cook the chicken over a high heat for 7–8 minutes until golden, crisp in places and cooked through. Remove from the pan with a slotted spoon and drain on kitchen paper before serving hot with mustard mayonnaise and a salad, if liked.

 2 Salt and Pepper Chicken Thighs with a Herby Coating Cut 8 chicken thighs, each about 125 g (4 oz), from the bone, and into 2 large pieces. Put 50 g (2 oz) plain flour in a bowl with 1 teaspoon black pepper, ½ teaspoon salt and 4 tablespoons chopped mixed herbs, such as parsley, thyme and rosemary. Toss the chicken in the seasoned flour to coat. Heat 4 tablespoons olive oil in a large, heavy-based frying pan and cook the chicken, turning once, over a high heat for 10 minutes. Reduce the heat and continue to cook for a further 5 minutes.

Paprika Chicken with Peppers

Serves 4

1 tablespoon sunflower oil
400 g (13 oz) mini-chicken fillets
1 teaspoon garlic paste
1 tablespoon paprika
175 g (6 oz) frozen sliced mixed
  peppers
1 tablespoon tomato purée
150 ml (¼ pint) soured cream
salt and pepper

- Heat the oil in large frying pan, add the chicken and stir-fry over a high heat for 5 minutes. Add the garlic paste, paprika, peppers and tomato purée and cook, stirring, for 3 minutes.

- Stir in the soured cream, season with salt and pepper and heat through. Serve with tagliatelle.

2   Paprika Chicken and Gnocchi Gratin

Prepare the Paprika Chicken with Peppers as above. When it is ready, stir in 400 g (13 oz) gnocchi, which have been cooked in lightly salted boiling water for 5 minutes and drained. Tip into a heatproof dish, sprinkle with 75 g (3 oz) grated Cheddar cheese and cook under a preheated grill for 5 minutes until the cheese is hot and bubbling.

3   Paprika Chicken Casserole

Fry 4 skinless chicken breast fillets in 1 tablespoon sunflower oil for 5 minutes, turning once, until golden. Add 1 chopped onion and 1 chopped green pepper, fry for 3 minutes then stir in 1 tablespoon paprika, 1 tablespoon tomato purée and 400 g (13 oz) can chopped tomatoes. Simmer for 15 minutes, season with salt and pepper and stir in 150 ml (¼ pint) soured cream. Serve with mashed potato.

 # Oriental Chicken Mince

Serves 4

250 g (8 oz) long grain rice
1 tablespoon sunflower oil
500 g (1 lb) chicken mince
6 spring onions, chopped
1 red chilli, deseeded and chopped
2 tablespoons black bean sauce
1 tablespoon light soy sauce
150 ml (¼ pint) chicken stock
1 teaspoon cornflour, mixed to
    smooth paste with a little water
salt and pepper

- Cook the rice in lightly salted boiling water for 10 minutes until tender, then drain.

- Meanwhile, heat the oil in a wok or large frying pan, add the chicken mince and fry, stirring, over a high heat for 5 minutes until it forms clumps.

- Add the spring onions and chilli and cook for 2 minutes. Stir in the black bean sauce, soy sauce and stock and simmer, stirring occasionally, for 5 minutes. Season with salt and pepper and pour in the cornflour paste. Cook, stirring, until thickened slightly. Serve with the cooked rice.

 Black Bean Mince with Prawn Crackers Stir-fry 500 g (1 lb) chicken mince in 1 tablespoon sunflower oil over a high heat for 5 minutes. Add 125 g (4 oz) ready-made black bean stir-fry sauce and cook for 3 minutes. Sprinkle with thinly sliced spring onions and serve with prawn crackers.

 Oriental Chicken Meatballs Mix 500 g (1 lb) chicken mince with 1 crushed garlic clove and season with salt and pepper. Roll the mixture into 24 small balls and fry in 2 tablespoons sunflower oil for 8–10 minutes or until golden and cooked. Remove from the pan. Fry 3 cored, deseeded and chopped mixed colour peppers and 1 onion, cut into wedges, for 5 minutes.

Drain 220 g (7½ oz) can pineapple chunks in natural juice, reserving the juice. Add the pineapple to the pan with the meatballs and stir in 3 tablespoons hoisin sauce, 1 tablespoon light soy sauce and 5 tablespoons of the reserved pineapple juice. Add 1 teaspoon cornflour mixed to a smooth paste with a little water and bring to the boil, stirring, until slightly thickened. Serve with rice.

30 Chicken and Rustic Chips

Serves 4

4 small baking potatoes, cut into
  chunky wedges
6 tablespoons olive oil
1 teaspoon salt flakes
4 chicken breast fillets, each
  about 150 g (5 oz)
2 tablespoons plain flour
½ teaspoon mustard powder
1 teaspoon black pepper
2 tablespoons chopped parsley
salt

- Coat the potato wedges in 4 tablespoons of the oil and toss with the salt flakes. Transfer to a baking sheet and roast in a preheated oven, 200°C (400°F), Gas Mark 6, for 20–25 minutes until golden in places.

- Meanwhile, cut each chicken breast in half across its width to make 2 thin chicken breasts. Put the flour in a large bowl with the mustard powder, pepper and parsley and season with a little salt. Mix well, add the chicken pieces and toss well to coat lightly in the seasoned flour.

- Heat the remaining oil in a large frying pan and cook the chicken, turning once, over a moderately high heat for 8–10 minutes until golden and cooked through. Serve the chicken with the roasted jacket wedges and with mayonnaise flavoured with mustard and a rocket salad, if liked.

---

1 **Seasoned Chicken Strips with Herby Mash** Toss 12 chicken mini-fillets in a bowl with 2 tablespoons plain flour and 1 teaspoon chicken seasoning. Heat 3 tablespoons olive oil in a large, heavy-based frying pan and cook the chicken over a high heat for 5 minutes until golden and cooked through. Serve with instant mashed potato with chopped parsley for colour and with 1 tablespoon crème fraîche per serving stirred through.

2 **Pan-Fried Chicken and Herby Cubed Potatoes** Chop 3 potatoes into small cubes. Heat 3 tablespoons olive oil in a large, heavy-based frying pan and cook the potatoes, stirring occasionally, over a moderately high heat for 12–15 minutes until golden and soft. Meanwhile, put 12 chicken mini-fillets in a bowl with 2 tablespoons plain flour, ½ teaspoon black pepper and ½ teaspoon mustard powder. Toss well to coat the fillets lightly. Heat a further 3 tablespoons olive oil in a separate frying pan and cook the chicken over a high heat for 8–20 minutes until golden and cooked through. Serve with the potatoes tossed in 3 tablespoons chopped parsley.

 # Chicken Curry in a Hurry

Serves 4

2 tablespoons sunflower oil
4 skinless chicken thigh fillets,
 chopped
2 sweet potatoes, peeled and
 cubed
3 tablespoons balti curry paste
400 g (13 oz) can chopped
 tomatoes
300 ml (½ pint) chicken stock
125 g (4 oz) frozen peas
small handful of fresh coriander
 leaves, roughly chopped
naan bread, to serve

- Heat the oil in a large frying pan, add the chicken and sweet potatoes and fry, stirring, over a high heat for 5 minutes.

- Add the curry paste, tomatoes and stock to the frying pan, bring to the boil, reduce the heat, cover and simmer for 10 minutes. Stir in the peas and cook for a further 5 minutes. Stir in the fresh coriander and serve with warm naan bread.

1 Curried Chicken Naans

Mix together 3 tablespoons mayonnaise, 2 teaspoons curry paste and 1 teaspoon tomato purée. Stir in 200 g (7 oz) chopped cooked chicken, 2 sliced celery sticks and ¼ chopped cucumber. Warm 4 small naan breads, top with Little Gem lettuce leaves and the curried chicken mixture.

3 Creamy Chicken Curry

Fry 1 sliced onion in 1 tablespoon sunflower oil for 5 minutes until softened. Add 4 chopped skinless chicken breast fillets and fry for 10 minutes. Stir in 125 g (4 oz) chopped no-need-to-soak apricots. Mix together 2 tablespoons medium curry paste, 300 g (10 oz) natural yogurt and 150 ml (¼ pint) double cream. Pour into the pan, bring the mixture to the boil and simmer for 5 minutes. Sprinkle with fresh coriander leaves and serve with rice.

CHI-MIDW-SOG

30 Chicken with Potatoes, Spinach and Blue Cheese

Serves 4

1 kg (2 lb) potatoes, roughly
  cubed
3 tablespoons vegetable oil
2 chicken breasts, each about
  150 g (5 oz), thinly sliced
2 teaspoons Cajun spice
250 g (8 oz) baby plum tomatoes
300 g (10 oz) fresh spinach
  leaves, washed and drained
125 g (4 oz) Danish blue cheese,
  crumbled

- Cook the potatoes in a large pan of lightly salted boiling water for 5 minutes. Drain well.

- Meanwhile, heat the oil in a large wok or frying pan and cook the chicken for 5 minutes over a high heat until golden and cooked. Remove from the pan with a slotted spoon and set aside. Add the drained potatoes to the pan and cook over a high heat for 10 minutes until golden and softened.

- Return the chicken to the pan with the Cajun spice and toss well to coat. Add the tomatoes and spinach leaves and toss and cook for 5 minutes, until the tomatoes have softened and the spinach has wilted.

- Crumble the cheese into the pan and remove from the heat. Toss lightly to allow the cheese to soften slightly, then spoon on to warmed serving plates.

 Chicken, Spinach and Blue Cheese Croquettes Make 100 g (3½ oz) instant mashed potato with boiling water or according to the instructions on the packet. Add 1 roughly chopped chicken breast and a handful of roughly chopped fresh spinach leaves. Stir in 50 g (2 oz) crumbled blue cheese. Shape into 4 croquettes and flatten slightly. Heat 3 tablespoons vegetable oil in a large, heavy-based frying pan and cook the croquettes over a high heat for 2 minutes on each side until golden. Serve with a green salad.

 Chicken, Spinach and Blue Cheese Rosti Cut 500 g (1 lb) potatoes in half and cook in a large pan of salted boiling water for 5 minutes. Drain, grate and put in a bowl with a large handful of shredded spinach, 50 g (2 oz) finely chopped cooked chicken and 50 g (2 oz) crumbled blue cheese. Mix together well and form into 4 patties. Heat 3 tablespoons vegetable oil in a large, heavy-based frying pan and cook the rosti for 2–3 minutes on each side until golden and crisp in places. Drain on kitchen paper and serve hot with a green salad.

10 Chicken and Sweetcorn Chowder

Serves 4

325 g (11 oz) can creamed
sweetcorn

450 ml (¾ pint) milk

175 g (6 oz) cooked chicken, torn
into pieces

125 g (4 oz) frozen sweetcorn
kernels

2 spring onions, chopped

2 teaspoons cornflour

salt and pepper

crusty bread, to serve

- Place the creamed sweetcorn in a saucepan with the milk and heat, stirring.

- Add the chicken, sweetcorn kernels and spring onions and season with salt and pepper. Simmer for 5 minutes, stirring occasionally.

- Blend the cornflour with 1 tablespoon water, pour into the soup and stir to thicken. Ladle into bowls and serve with crusty bread.

2 Chicken and Sweetcorn Fritters

Mix together 100 g (3½ oz) plain flour, 1 teaspoon baking powder, a little salt and pepper, 1 egg and 150 ml (¼ pint) milk to make smooth batter. Stir in 200 g (7 oz) can drained sweetcorn and 175 g (6 oz) chopped cooked chicken. Fry large spoonfuls of the mixture in 1 tablespoon sunflower oil for 2 minutes on each side until golden. Serve with crispy bacon rashers and tomato ketchup.

3 Chicken, Bacon and Sweetcorn Chowder

Fry 2 chopped rashers of bacon with 1 chopped onion and 2 chopped medium potatoes in a knob of butter for 5 minutes. Pour in 500 ml (17 fl oz) milk and simmer for 10 minutes. Stir in 125 g (4 oz) frozen sweetcorn kernels and 175 g (6 oz) chopped cooked chicken. Season with salt and pepper, heat through and serve sprinkled with chopped fresh parsley.

30 Chicken Thighs with Spinach, Lemon and Ricotta Filling

Serves 4

8 skinless chicken thighs, each
   about 125 g (4 oz)
1 tablespoon olive oil
200 g (7 oz) fresh spinach leaves,
   washed and drained
1 teaspoon ground nutmeg
finely grated rind of 1 lemon
125 g (4 oz) ricotta cheese
salt and pepper

- Unroll the chicken thighs on a board and season well with a little salt and plenty of black pepper.

- Heat the oil in a pan and cook the spinach over a moderate heat for 2 minutes, stirring continually until wilted. Remove from the heat and drain well, pressing the leaves into a sieve to remove any excess liquid. Roughly chop the spinach. Place in a bowl and add the nutmeg and lemon rind. Season with pepper. Stir in the ricotta until well blended.

- Put spoonfuls of the mixture in the centre of the chicken thighs and roll up loosely so that filling does not come out, holding the chicken together with cocktail sticks.

- Transfer to a roasting tin and bake in a preheated oven, 200°C (400°F), Gas Mark 6, for 15 minutes or until cooked. Serve hot with a simple salad and warm crusty bread.

1 Chicken with Ricotta, Sun-Dried Tomato and Pine Nuts

Cut 4 chicken breast fillets, each about 125 (4 oz), almost in half widthways and open out. Heat 1 tablespoon olive oil in a large pan and cook the chicken, turning once, for 7–8 minutes or until cooked through. Meanwhile, in a small pan mix together 125 g (4 oz) ricotta cheese, ½ teaspoon nutmeg, the finely grated rind of 1 lemon and 2 tablespoons toasted pine nuts. Stir in 5 chopped sun-dried tomatoes and 2 tablespoons milk and gently heat. Serve spooned over the chicken.

2 Chicken with Ricotta, Sun-Dried Tomato and Basil

Mix together 125 g (4 oz) ricotta cheese, 8 roughly chopped sun-dried tomatoes and 3 tablespoons chopped basil. Cut 4 chicken breasts, each about 125 g (4 oz), in half across their width and fill each with spoonfuls of the ricotta mixture. Hold together with cocktail sticks. Heat 2 tablespoons olive oil in a large, heavy-based frying pan and cook the chicken over a moderately high heat for 5 minutes on each side. Cover with a lid and cook for a further 3 minutes. Serve hot with a simple watercress salad and warm crusty bread, if liked.

 Chicken Chilli Pasta

Serves 4

1 tablespoon sunflower oil
500 g (1 lb) chicken mince
1 garlic clove, crushed
1 teaspoon chilli powder
½ teaspoon chilli flakes
450 ml (¾ pint) passata
1 tablespoon sun-dried tomato
 pesto
375 g (12 oz) spaghetti
salt and pepper
freshly grated Parmesan cheese,
 to serve

- Heat the oil in a large frying pan, add the chicken mince and fry over a high heat for 5 minutes, breaking up any clumps.

- Add the garlic, chilli powder, chilli flakes, passata and pesto. Season with salt and pepper, bring to the boil, then reduce the heat and simmer for 10 minutes.

- Meanwhile, cook the spaghetti in lightly salted boiling water for 8–10 minutes or until just tender. Drain and toss with the chicken chilli sauce. Serve with plenty of freshly grated Parmesan cheese.

---

1 Chilli Chicken with Tortilla Chips

Heat 350 g (11½ oz) ready-made tomato and chilli pasta sauce in a saucepan. Add 220 g (7½ oz) can rinsed and drained red kidney beans and 175 g (6 oz) chopped cooked chicken and heat through. Serve with soured cream and tortilla chips.

3 Baked Chilli Chicken

Cut several slashes across the top of 4 chicken breast fillets (with skin on). Place in a foil-lined baking tin and pour over a mixture of 5 tablespoons balsamic vinegar, 2 tablespoons lemon juice, 4 tablespoons olive oil and 1 chopped red chilli. Bake in a preheated oven, 200°C (400°F), Gas Mark 6, for 25 minutes with 500 g (1 lb) frozen roast potatoes in a separate baking tin until the chicken is cooked and the potatoes are crisp. Serve with peas.

3 ◐ Chicken, Broccoli and Cheese Bake

Serves 4

2 tablespoons olive oil

3 chicken breasts, each about
  150 g (5 oz), thinly sliced

300 g (10 oz) broccoli florets

500 g (1 lb) pot of ready-made
  fresh cheese sauce

1 teaspoon grated nutmeg

¼ ciabatta loaf, torn into
  bite-sized pieces

4 tablespoons olive oil

½ teaspoon salt flakes

½ teaspoon black pepper

2 tablespoons fresh chopped
  parsley

4 tablespoons freshly grated
  Parmesan cheese

- Preheat the oven to 200°C (400°F), Gas Mark 6. Heat the oil in a large, heavy-based frying pan or wok and cook the chicken pieces for 5 minutes, stirring occasionally, until golden and cooked.

- Meanwhile, put the broccoli in a pan of lightly salted boiling water and cook for 5 minutes or until just tender. Drain and toss with the cooked chicken. Pour in the cheese sauce, add the nutmeg and toss well to coat. Cook, stirring occasionally, for 2–3 minutes until hot. Transfer to a shallow heatproof gratin dish, or 4 individual gratin dishes.

- Meanwhile, put the bread in a large bowl with the oil and toss well. Add the salt, pepper and herbs and toss again.

- Scatter the bread pieces over the chicken mixture and scatter with the Parmesan. Cook for 15 minutes in the top of the oven until golden and bubbling. Serve with a simple salad, if liked.

---

1 ◐ Chicken, Broccoli and Cheese Soup

Put 250 g (8 oz) broccoli florets in 300 ml (½ pint) boiling water, cover with a tight-fitting lid and cook for 5 minutes. Add 500 g (1 lb) pot of ready-made fresh cheese sauce, 125 g (4 oz) cooked chicken and ½ teaspoon grated nutmeg. Bring to the boil then transfer to a food processor or blender and process until smooth.

2 ◐ Chicken, Broccoli and Cheese Gratin

Make the chicken, broccoli, sauce and nutmeg mixture as above and heat until piping hot. Spoon the mixture into 4 individual gratin dishes. Mix together 75 g (3 oz) breadcrumbs and 2 tablespoons freshly grated Parmesan cheese and scatter evenly over each gratin dish. Place under a preheated hot grill and cook for 5 minutes until piping hot and golden in places. Serve with a simple salad.

30 Smoky Cannellini Bean Stew with Sausages and Chicken

Serves 4

1 tablespoon olive oil
4 good quality pork sausages
300 g (10 oz) chicken, roughly diced
1 red onion, sliced
1 red pepper, cored, deseeded and cut into strips
100 g (3½ oz) chorizo sausage, sliced
2 teaspoons smoked paprika
2 × 400 g (13 oz) cans cannellini beans, rinsed and drained
400 g (13 oz) can chopped tomatoes
600 ml (1 pint) chicken stock
1 tablespoon cornflour
4 tablespoons chopped parsley

- Heat the oil in a large, heavy-based frying pan and cook the sausages over a moderate heat, turning occasionally, for 10 minutes until golden and cooked through. Remove from the pan with a slotted spoon and transfer to kitchen paper to cool and drain.

- Add the chicken to the pan and stir-fry for 3 minutes. Add the onion and pepper to the pan and cook for 3 minutes more before adding the chorizo and cooking for a further 2 minutes. Stir in the smoked paprika. Add the beans, tomatoes and stock and bring to the boil. Cut the sausages into thick chunks and add to the pan. Reduce the heat and cover and simmer for 10 minutes.

- Blend the cornflour with 2 tablespoons water and add to the pan with the parsley and stir well until thickened slightly.

- Ladle the stew into warm bowls and serve with crusty bread to mop up the juices.

---

10 Smoky Chicken and Beans on Toast

Heat 1 tablespoon olive oil in a frying pan and cook 2 thinly sliced chicken breasts, each about 150 g (5 oz), for 3–4 minutes over a high heat. Add 1 teaspoon smoked paprika, 300 g (10 oz) jar drained antipasti roasted peppers, 400 g (13 oz) can cannellini beans and 400 g (13 oz) can chopped tomatoes. Bring to the boil and cook for 3 minutes or until piping hot. Serve on warm thick toast.

20 Smoky Chicken and Bean Stew

Heat 1 tablespoon olive oil in a large saucepan and cook 1 sliced onion and 2 thinly sliced chicken breasts, each about 150 g (5 oz), for 3–4 minutes. Add 1 thinly sliced red pepper and 1 thinly sliced courgette and cook for 2–3 minutes. Add 2 teaspoons smoked paprika, stir and add 2 × 400 g (13 oz) cans cannellini beans and 600 ml (1 pint) chicken stock and bring to the boil. Reduce the heat and simmer for 5 minutes before adding 4 teaspoons cornflour blended with 2 tablespoons water. Stir well to thicken. Serve with crusty bread.

CHI-MIDW-VYT

QuickCook

Family
Favourites

Recipes listed by cooking time

30

20

1

3 Roasted Chicken Thighs with Roots and Honey

Serves 4

4 chicken thighs
4 small parsnips, each quartered
  lengthways
4 large carrots, each quartered
  lengthways
3 tablespoons olive oil
3 tablespoons clear honey
pepper
4 tablespoons chopped parsley,
  to garnish

- Put the chicken thighs in a roasting tin with the parsnips and carrots. Drizzle over the olive oil and shake the vegetables and chicken to coat in the oil. Season generously with pepper and roast in a preheated oven, 220°C (425°F), Gas Mark 7, for 20–25 minutes or until golden, drizzling over the honey for the final 3 minutes of cooking.

- Scatter over the parsley serve with instant mashed potatoes and a green vegetable, if liked.

---

1 Sticky Chicken and Carrot Stir-Fry with Honey and Thyme

Heat 2 tablespoons olive oil and cook 375 g (12 oz) diced chicken meat over a high heat for 2 minutes to seal. Add 2 large thinly sliced carrots and stir-fry for 6–7 minutes or until the chicken and carrots are cooked through. Drizzle over 4 tablespoons clear honey and 1 tablespoon thyme leaves and toss to coat. Serve with instant mashed potato or express rice.

2 Honeyed Chicken Breasts with Baby Carrots, Parsnips and Thyme

Heat 2 tablespoons olive oil in a large, heavy-based frying pan and cook 4 chicken breasts, each 75–125 g (3–4 oz), over a high heat for 2 minutes on each side to seal. Add 175 g (6 oz) baby carrots and 2 roughly chopped parsnips and cook over a high heat, turning all the ingredients occasionally, for 10 minutes or until golden and cooked through. Season generously with pepper. Add 2 tablespoons clear honey and stir through. Garnish with 1 tablespoon thyme leaves.

30 Chicken Biryani

Serves 4

250 g (8 oz) easy-cook
  basmati rice
2 tablespoons oil
1 large onion, thinly sliced
300 g (10 oz) diced chicken
1 bay leaf
3 cardamom pods
1 teaspoon turmeric
4 tablespoons curry paste
150 ml (¼ pint) chicken stock
75 g (3 oz) raisins
4 tablespoons natural yogurt
50 g (2 oz) toasted flaked
  almonds
4 tablespoons chopped fresh
  coriander, to garnish

- Cook the rice in a large saucepan of lightly salted boiling water for 15–20 minutes or until tender.

- Meanwhile, heat the oil in a large, heavy-based frying pan and cook the onion and chicken over a moderately high heat for 5–8 minutes or until golden, adding the bay leaf, cardamom and turmeric for the final 1 minute of cooking.

- Add the curry paste and stir-fry for 1 minute, then pour in the stock. Bring to the boil, add the raisins and yogurt and cook gently for 10 minutes, until the stock has reduced by half.

- Drain the cooked rice, add to the pan with the chicken and toss and cook for 2–3 minutes. Scatter with flaked almonds and garnish with chopped fresh coriander.

1 Simple Fruity Chicken Biryani

Cook 250 g (8 oz) express rice and set aside. Heat 1 tablespoon oil in a heavy-based frying pan and cook 250 g (8 oz) diced chicken over a high heat for 8 minutes or until golden. Add 2 tablespoons curry paste, 75 g (3 oz) raisins and 4 tablespoons flaked almonds and toss well in the pan. Add the cooked rice and toss again before garnishing with fresh coriander to serve.

2 Green Chicken Biryani

Cook 175 g (6 oz) easy-cook long grain rice in a large saucepan of lightly salted boiling water and cook for 10–12 minutes or until tender. Heat 2 tablespoons oil in a large, heavy-based frying pan and cook 250 g (8 oz) diced chicken with 8 tablespoons chopped fresh coriander for 5–8 minutes or until golden in places. Add 3 tablespoons curry paste and stir-fry for 3 minutes before adding 400 g (13 oz) can spinach leaf. Reduce the heat and cook for 3–4 minutes or until piping hot. Drain the rice well and add to the pan with the chicken and spinach, toss well over the heat and serve.

Tomato, Chicken, Pepper and Olive Tuscan-Style Tarts

Serves 4

375 g (12 oz) ready-rolled puff
pastry
2 tomatoes, sliced
150 g (5 oz) spicy tomato-
flavoured chicken slices
8 small pepper pieces, drained
from an antipasti pepper jar
1 tablespoon thyme leaves
125 g (4 oz) kalamata olives,
drained
1 tablespoon olive oil
salt and pepper
green salad, to serve

- Unroll the ready-rolled puff pastry, cut it into 4 x 12 cm (5 inch) circles and place well spaced apart on a large baking sheet. Prick the bases all over with a fork.

- Arrange the tomato slices randomly on top of each one, dividing them evenly between the bases and keeping a 1 cm (½ inch) border around the edge. Evenly scatter over the chicken slices, peppers, thyme and olives, then drizzle with the olive oil and season with salt and pepper.

- Bake at the top of a preheated oven, 220°C (425°F), Gas Mark 7, for 12–15 minutes or until the pastry is puffed and golden and the topping soft. Serve the tarts with a simple green salad.

Savoury Chicken and Pepper Croustades Halve 2 foccacia rolls. Drizzle each side with 1 tablespoon olive oil and cook under a preheated grill for 2 minutes or until warm. Set aside wrapped in foil to keep warm. Place 150 g (5 oz) sliced chicken breast in a pan with 300 g (10 oz) jar roasted red peppers, drained and sliced, and 4 tablespoons kalamata olives. Warm through over a gentle heat, stirring occasionally, for 4–5 minutes or until hot. Add 3 tablespoons chopped parsley and stir through. Serve spooned over the warm toasted foccacia slices.

Tuscan Tart with Artichokes and Lemon Unroll 375 g (12 oz) sheet of ready-rolled puff pastry on a large baking sheet. Scatter over 400 g (13 oz) well-drained jar of artichokes mixed with the finely grated rind of 1 lemon and 4 tablespoons chopped parsley. Toss 150 g (5 oz) cooked spicy tomato chicken slices with 1 tablespoon of the artichoke oil or 1 tablespoon olive oil and scatter over the top with 1 chopped tomato and 125 g (4 oz) drained kalamata olives. Bake in a preheated oven, 220°C (425°F), Gas Mark 7, for 25 minutes or until well puffed and golden.

Chicken and Boston Beans

Serves 4

1 tablespoon olove oil

2 chicken breasts, each about
150 g (5 oz), thinly sliced

1 onion, thinly sliced

1 tablespoon black treacle

1 tablespoon wholegrain mustard

1 tablespoon soft dark brown
sugar

400 g (13 oz) can chopped
tomatoes

400 g (13 oz) can baked beans

3 tablespoons chopped parsley

pepper

wholemeal toast, to serve

· Heat the oil in a medium-sized, heavy-based saucepan
and cook the chicken and onion over a moderate heat for
3–4 minutes.

· Add the treacle, mustard, sugar and tomatoes, bring to the
boil and simmer for 2 minutes before adding the beans, then
stir in the parsley and heat through for 1 minute.

· Spoon the mixture on to 4 warm thick slices of wholemeal
toast, season with pepper and serve immediately.

---

2 **Paprika Boston
Baked Beans with
Chicken and Bacon** Heat 2
tablespoons olive oil in a large,
frying pan and cook 1 thinly sliced
onion, 2 thinly sliced chicken
breasts and 4 rashers of chopped
streaky bacon for 5 minutes or
until golden, soft and cooked
through. Add 1 teaspoon paprika,
1 tablespoon treacle, 1 tablespoon
wholegrain mustard and
2 tablespoons soft dark brown
sugar and stir well. Stir in 400 g
(13 oz) can chopped tomatoes and
2 × 400 g (13 oz) cans cannellini
beans. Bring to the boil, cover
and simmer for 10 minutes,
removing the lid for the final 2
minutes. Stir through 2 tablespoons
chopped parsley and serve.

3 **Cannellini Boston
Bean Gratin**
Heat 2 tablespoons olive oil in a
large, heavy-based frying pan
and cook 1 large thinly sliced
onion and 2 thinly sliced chicken
breasts, each about 150 g (5 oz),
over a moderately high heat for
5 minutes. Add 2 tablespoons
treacle, 1 tablespoon wholegrain
mustard and 1 tablespoon soft
dark brown sugar, 400 g (13 oz)
can chopped tomatoes and
2 × 400 g (13 oz) cans cannellini
beans. Bring to the boil and
simmer for 8–10 minutes or
until the mixture has thickened.
Transfer to a large, shallow
gratin dish. In a bowl mix
together 125 g (4 oz) wholemeal
breadcrumbs, 50 g (2 oz) freshly

grated Parmesan cheese and
2 tablespoons chopped parsley
and scatter evenly over the
beans and up to the edges of
the dish. Put under a preheated
moderately hot grill for 3–4
minutes or until the topping is
golden and melted. Serve with
a simple salad and bread to mop
up the juices.

CHI-FAMI-COO

Spicy Chicken Wings with Avocado Salsa

Serves 4

2 tablespoons oil
4 tablespoons tomato ketchup
3 tablespoons sweet chilli sauce
½ teaspoon chilli flakes
1 tablespoon clear honey
½ teaspoons ground black pepper
750 g (1½ lb) chicken wings

For the avocado salsa

1 avocado, chopped
125 g (4 oz) cherry plum
  tomatoes, quartered
2 tablespoons fresh chopped
  coriander
finely grated rind and juice
  of 1 lime
1 teaspoon olive oil
ground black pepper

- Mix together the oil, ketchup, chilli sauce, chilli flakes, honey and pepper in a large mixing bowl, add the chicken wings and stir well to coat each in the mixture.

- Arrange the wings in a single layer on a foil-lined grill rack and cook under a preheated hot grill for 10 minutes on one side, before turning and cooking for 5–7 minutes on the other until the chicken is cooked through.

- Meanwhile, make the avocado salsa by mixing together all the salsa ingredients in a small bowl and seasoning generously with pepper. Serve the chicken piping hot with the salsa separately and crusty bread to mop up the juices, if liked.

 Spicy Chicken Cubes with Guacamole Mix together the ketchup, chilli sauce, chilli flakes, honey and pepper as above in a mixing bowl. Add 375 g (12 oz) chicken breast cubes and 100 g (3½ oz) cherry tomatoes and toss well to coat. Place on a foil-lined grill rack and cook under a preheated hot grill, turning once, for 7–8 minutes or until lightly charred in places and cooked through. Serve with spoonfuls of ready-made guacamole.

Roasted Chicken Wings with Barbecue Sauce and Griddled Peppers Mix together 4 tablespoons tomato ketchup, 4 tablespoons soft brown sugar and 1 tablespoon red wine vinegar. Add 3 tablespoons clear honey and mix well. Add 750 g (1½ lb) small chicken wings and toss to coat in the mixture. Arrange the wings in a single layer in a roasting tin and cook in a preheated oven, 220°C (425°F), Gas Mark 7, for 25 minutes or until cooked through and lightly charred in places. Meanwhile, cut 1 red and 1 orange pepper into large chunks. Heat 1 tablespoon olive oil on a griddle pan and cook the peppers for 5–10 minutes or until lightly charred and softened. Toss with the barbecued chicken and serve with rice, if liked, and with any remaining juices from the pan spooned over the chicken.

CHI-FAMI-TET

30 Chicken, Bacon and Mushroom Pie

Serves 4

3 tablespoons olive oil
375 g (12 oz) diced chicken
175 g (6 oz) diced bacon
250 g (8 oz) chestnut
    mushrooms, halved
75 g (3 oz) butter
25 g (1 oz) plain flour
300 ml (½ pint) milk
2 tablespoons wholegrain
    mustard
4 tablespoons chopped parsley
2 tablespoons thyme leaves
125 g (4 oz) packet instant
    mashed potato
2 tablespoons freshly grated
    Parmesan cheese
salt and pepper

· Heat 1 tablespoon of the oil in a large frying pan and cook the chicken and bacon pieces over a high heat for 8–10 minutes or until golden. Meanwhile, in a separate pan, heat the remaining oil and cook the mushrooms over a high heat, stirring, for 5 minutes or until golden and soft. Mix the cooked mushrooms with the bacon and chicken.

· In a medium-sized saucepan melt 50 g (2 oz) of the butter, stir in the flour and cook for 1 minute. Remove from the heat and add the milk a little at a time, stirring between each addition until blended. Return to the heat and stir until boiled and thickened. Stir in the mustard and season, then set aside.

· Add the parsley and half the thyme to the chicken and bacon. Pour in the sauce, mix and transfer to a shallow gratin dish.

· Make up the potato mix according to the instructions on the packet. Add the remaining butter and thyme and beat well to fluff up. Spoon over the chicken and bacon mixture and scatter with the Parmesan. Cook under the preheated grill for 3–4 minutes or until golden and bubbling.

10 Creamy Chicken and Bacon Pan-Fry

with Spinach Heat 1 tablespoon olive oil in a large, heavy-based frying pan and cook 250 g (8 oz) diced chicken with 250 g (8 oz) diced bacon over a high heat for 7–8 minutes or until golden. Add 300 g (10 oz) washed spinach leaves and stir-fry with the chicken for 2 minutes before adding 200 ml (7 fl oz) crème fraîche with 1 tablespoon wholegrain mustard. Heat for 1 minute over a high heat until piping hot. Serve with warm crusty bread.

20 Creamy Chicken, Mushroom and

Bacon Pan-Fry with Herby Mash Heat 2 tablespoons olive oil in a large frying pan and cook 375 g (12 oz) diced chicken with 250 g (8 oz) diced bacon pieces over a high heat for 8–10 minutes or until golden and cooked through. In a separate wok or heavy-based frying pan heat 2 tablespoons olive oil and cook 250 g (8 oz) halved chestnut mushrooms for 8–10 minutes or until golden and soft. Add the chicken to the mushrooms and add 400 ml (14 fl oz) crème fraîche, 1 tablespoon thyme leaves and 1 tablespoon wholegrain mustard. Serve hot ladled on to 125 g (4 oz) instant mashed potato made according to the instructions on the packet and mixed with 1 tablespoon thyme leaves.

20 Flattened Chicken with Prosciutto and Gruyère

Serves 4

4 chicken breasts, each about
    125 g (4 oz)
1 egg, beaten
125 g (4 oz) fresh white
    breadcrumbs
4 tablespoons olive oil
4 slices of Gruyère cheese
4 slices of prosciutto
sage leaves, to garnish

- Put the chicken breasts between 2 sheets of oiled clingfilm and beat with a rolling pin until almost doubled in size. Place the beaten egg on a plate and the breadcrumbs on a separate plate. Lightly coat each chicken breast in egg and then in the breadcrumbs. Set aside.

- Heat the oil in a large, heavy-based frying pan. (You may need to use 2 pans so that you can cook all the chicken at the same time.) Cook the chicken over a moderate heat for 4 minutes on each side or until golden and crisp.

- Transfer to 2 baking sheets and and top with Gruyère cheese slices and a slice of prosciutto. Grill under a hot preheated grill for 2 minutes, then turn off the heat and leave to stand for a further 2 minutes or until the cheese has melted a little. Serve garnished with sage leaves.

10 Crunchy Chicken Gougons with Warm Gruyère Sauce

Lightly toss 500 g (1 lb) mini-breast fillets in 75 g (3 oz) fresh white breadcrumbs. Heat 8 tablespoons olive oil in a large, heavy-based frying pan and cook the chicken, turning occasionally, over a medium heat for 7–8 minutes or until golden and cooked through. Meanwhile, put 75 g (3 oz) grated Gruyère cheese in a small pan with 200 ml (7 fl oz) crème fraîche and 2 teaspoons Dijon mustard. Warm through gently, stirring with a wooden spoon, until the cheese melts. Serve the gougons with the cheese sauce to dip into.

30 Chicken, Gruyère and Prosciutto Rolls

Flatten 4 chicken breasts, each about 125 g (4 oz), between 2 sheets of oiled clingfilm until thin and almost doubled in size. Grate 75 g (3 oz) Gruyère cheese and sprinkle evenly over the top of each chicken breast. Season generously with plenty of pepper, top with a slice of prosciutto and scatter with 2 tablespoons chopped sage. Roll up each chicken breast tightly to form a neat roll and secure with a cocktail stick. Heat 2 tablespoons olive oil in a large, heavy-based frying pan (with a lid) and cook the chicken rolls, turning occasionally, over a moderately high heat for 10 minutes or until evenly golden. Cover with a lid for the final 10 minutes of cooking and reduce to a gentle heat. Serve with a simple salad.

Thick Curried Coconut and Spinach Soup

Serves 4

2 chicken breasts, each about
 150 g (5 oz), thinly sliced
1 teaspoon ground coriander
250 g (8 oz) packets express rice
2 × 400 ml (14 fl oz) cans
 coconut milk
2 tablespoons korma curry paste
300 ml (½ pint) chicken stock
6 tablespoons chopped fresh
 coriander
300 g (10 oz) fresh spinach,
 washed and drained
salt and pepper
naan bread, to serve

• Put the sliced chicken in a large saucepan with the ground coriander, rice, coconut milk, curry paste and stock and bring to the boil. Cover and simmer for 5 minutes.

• Add the fresh coriander and spinach leaves and continue to cook, stirring occasionally, for 2–3 minutes more or until the spinach has wilted. Season generously with salt and pepper, ladle into warmed serving bowls and serve with warm naan bread.

Hot and Spicy Chicken and Coconut Soup with Okra Put 2 thinly sliced chicken breasts, each about 150 g (5 oz), in a saucepan with 2 × 400 ml (14 fl oz) cans coconut milk, 2 tablespoons hot curry paste, 1 thinly sliced bird's eye chilli, 3 tablespoons chopped fresh coriander, 250 g (8 oz) roughly chopped okra and 300 ml (½ pint) rich chicken stock. Bring to the boil and cook for 15 minutes or until piping hot and the okra is tender. Ladle into warmed serving bowls and serve with warm naan bread.

Thick Lentil, Coconut and Spinach Soup Put 2 thinly sliced chicken breasts, each about 150 g (5 oz), in a large, heavy-based saucepan with 175 g (6 oz) red lentils, 2 teaspoons ground coriander, 2 × 400 ml (14 fl oz) cans coconut milk, 2 tablespoons korma curry paste, 1 bunch of chopped spring onions and 300 ml (½ pint) chicken stock and bring to the boil. Reduce the heat, cover and simmer, stirring occasionally, for 20–25 minutes or until the lentils are tender, adding 300 g (10 oz) fresh spinach leaves for the final 5 minutes of cooking. Serve with warm naan bread.

30 Chicken, Bacon, Vegetable and Cheese Layers

Serves 4

4 tablespoons olive oil

2 chicken breasts, each about 150 g (5 oz), thinly sliced

175 g (6 oz) streaky bacon, chopped

375 g (12 oz) butternut squash, thinly sliced

1 red onion, thinly sliced

4 large tomatoes, sliced

150 g (5 oz) mature Cheddar cheese, grated

4 tablespoons chopped parsley (optional)

- Heat the oil in a large, heavy-based frying pan and cook the chicken breasts and bacon over a high heat for 3 minutes. Add the thinly sliced butternut squash and onion and continue cooking over a high heat for 10 minutes.

- Put a layer of one-half of the sliced tomatoes in the base of a shallow, ovenproof dish. Spoon half the chicken and butternut mixture over the top. Scatter over one-half of the grated cheese. Top with a further layer of tomatoes and the remaining chicken and butternut and a layer of cheese.

- Cook under a preheated moderate grill for 10–15 minutes or until golden and bubbling. Garnish with parsley, if liked, and serve with a simple crisp green salad.

1 Chicken, Tomato and Cheese Layers

Slice 6 tomatoes and layer in 4 individual shallow gratin dishes with 175 g (6 oz) sliced cooked chicken pieces, 6 tablespoons chopped parsley and 175 g (6 oz) grated Cheddar cheese, finishing with a layer of cheese. Put the dishes on a baking sheet and cook under a preheated hot grill for 1 minute or until golden and softened. Serve with crusty bread.

2 Butternut Squash, Bacon and Chicken Pan-Fry with Artichokes

Heat 1 tablespoon olive oil and 25 g (1 oz) butter in a large, heavy-based frying pan and cook 250 g (8 oz) diced chicken and 125 g (4 oz) diced bacon pieces over a high heat for 5 minutes. Meanwhile, thinly slice 350 g (11½ oz) butternut squash. Add the squash to the pan and cook, stirring frequently, for a further 10 minutes or until the squash is golden and softened. Drain and quarter 400 g (13 oz) can artichoke hearts, add to the pan and cook for 2 minutes or until hot. Scatter over 6–8 tablespoons chopped flat leaf parsley and serve on warmed serving plates with freshly grated Parmesan cheese, if liked.

30 Speedy Roast Chicken with Bacon and Stuffing

Serves 4

4 chicken breasts, each about
125 g (4 oz)
50 g (2 oz) sage and onion
stuffing mix
4 bacon rashers
250 g (8 oz) baby carrots
3 tablespoons olive oil
2 tablespoons chopped parsley

- Put the chicken breasts on a board and slice them lengthways almost all the way through, leaving a 'hinge' at one long end. Make up the stuffing mix according to the instructions on the packet and use 1 tablespoon of the stuffing to fill each of the breasts. Wrap each tightly with a bacon rasher to keep the stuffing in place.

- Put the chicken and carrots in 1 or 2 roasting tins, drizzle over the oil and shake gently to coat in the oil. Roast in a preheated oven, 200°C (400°F), Gas Mark 6, for 25 minutes or until the chicken is golden and cooked through. Scatter over the parsley to garnish before serving.

10 Simple Chicken and Bacon Pan-Fry with Sage and Onion

Heat 3 tablespoons olive oil in a large, heavy-based frying pan and cook 1 roughly sliced red onion, 375 g (12 oz) chicken mini-fillets and 4 roughly chopped back bacon rashers over a high heat, stirring occasionally, for 8–10 minutes or until golden and soft. Add 1 tablespoon chopped sage leaves and cook for a few more seconds before serving with instant mashed potatoes and chicken gravy, if liked.

20 Pan-Fried Chicken Wrapped in Bacon with Stuffing Balls

Tightly wrap 4 chicken breasts, each about 125 g (4 oz), in 4 back bacon rashers. Heat 2 tablespoons olive oil in a large, heavy-based frying pan and cook the chicken over a high heat, join side down, for 5 minutes, then turn and cook for a further 5 minutes. Meanwhile, make up 75 g (3 oz) sage and onion stuffing according to the instructions on the packet and shape into 4 balls. Add to the pan, reduce the heat and cover and simmer for 5 minutes. Serve garnished with 2 tablespoons chopped flat leaf parsley.

20 Simple Chicken Korma

Serves 4

2 tablespoons oil
1 large onion, roughly chopped
500 g (1 lb) chicken breast, diced
1 teaspoon minced ginger
1 teaspoon minced garlic
1 teaspoon dried chilli flakes
1 tablespoon ground coriander
1 teaspoon ground turmeric
1 teaspoon ground garam masala
4 tablespoons ground almonds
300 g (10 oz) natural yogurt
300 ml (½ pint) double cream
6 tablespoons chopped fresh
  coriander
plain rice, to serve

- Heat the oil in a large, heavy-based frying pan and cook the onion and chicken for 5 minutes or until softened and golden in places. Add all the spices and cook over a high heat for 2–3 minutes, tossing and stirring until well blended.

- Add the ground almonds and stir to coat, then pour in the yogurt and cream. Cook, uncovered and stirring occasionally, over a gentle heat for 10 minutes or until the chicken is cooked and the sauce is well coloured and a good consistency, adding a little water if necessary. Remove from the heat, stir in the fresh coriander and serve with rice, if liked.

10 Quick Chicken Korma

Heat 2 tablespoons oil in a large, heavy-based frying pan and cook 500 g (1 lb) diced chicken over a high heat, stirring occasionally, for 5 minutes or until golden in places. Add 3 tablespoons korma curry paste and cook for a few seconds before adding 300 g (10 oz) natural yogurt and 8 tablespoons double cream. Cook over a moderately high heat for 4–5 minutes or until the sauce has reduced slightly and the chicken is cooked through. Serve with warm naan bread.

30 Chicken and Potato Korma with Spinach

Cut 2 potatoes, each about 175 g (6 oz), into chunks. Heat 2 tablespoons oil in a large, heavy-based saucepan and cook 1 large chopped onion, 375 g (12 oz) diced chicken and the potatoes over a high heat for 5 minutes or until golden in places. Add 1 chopped garlic clove, 1 teaspoon minced ginger and the chilli flakes, ground coriander, turmeric and garam masala as above. Cook for 2 minutes. Add 5 tablespoons ground almonds and 400 ml (14 fl oz) can coconut milk, bring to the boil, reduce the heat and simmer, stirring occasionally, for 15 minutes. Stir in 300 g (10 oz) natural yogurt and cook for a further 5 minutes, stirring occasionally, until the potatoes are tender and the chicken is cooked. Stir in 400 g (13 oz) can spinach leaf and 4 tablespoons chopped fresh coriander and heat for 2 minutes more before serving.

CHI-FAMI-WUE

30 Barbecue Poussin Pieces with Corn and Chilli Salsa

Serves 4

2 poussins, each jointed in half
finely grated rind and juice of
  1 lime
1 tablespoon Cajun spice mix
2 tablespoons olive oil
175 g (6 oz) can sweetcorn
1 red chilli, finely chopped
¼ cucumber, finely chopped
salt and pepper

- Put the jointed poussins in a large roasting tin and season all over with salt and pepper. Mix together the lime rind and juice, Cajun spice and 1 tablespoon of the olive oil and use to brush over the poussin pieces. Cook on a hot barbecue, turning occasionally, for 25 minutes or until golden in places and cooked through.

- Meanwhile, put the sweetcorn in a mixing bowl with the chilli, cucumber and the remaining olive oil. Toss together well and serve with the cooked poussin pieces.

 Spicy Pan-Fried Chicken with Chilli and Corn Heat 2 tablespoons olive oil in a large, heavy-based frying pan or wok. Toss 375 g (12 oz) diced chicken with 1 teaspoon Cajun spice and 1 finely chopped red chilli and stir-fry in the pan over a high heat for 5 minutes or until golden. Add 175 g (6 oz) can drained sweetcorn and 175 g (6 oz) sugar snap peas and continue to cook for 3 minutes, stirring continually. Serve in warmed serving bowls with wedges of lime to squeeze over.

 Barbecued Chicken Kebabs with Corn and Chilli Salsa Cut 3 chicken breasts, each about 150 g (5 oz), into cubes and place in a bowl with 1 tablespoon olive oil and 2 teaspoons Cajun spice and toss well. Thread the chicken on to 4 bamboo or metal kebab skewers and cook on a hot barbecue for 10–12 minutes or until lightly charred and cooked through. Meanwhile, make the salsa as above and serve with the hot kebabs.

10 Warm Chicken Ciabatta with Salsa and Rocket

Serves 4

1 tablespoon olive oil
2 chicken breasts, each about
  150 g (5 oz), sliced lengthways
1 ciabatta loaf, halved
2 ripe tomatoes, roughly chopped
1 small red onion, thinly sliced
3 tablespoons chopped parsley
mayonnaise, to taste
mustard, to taste
pepper
rocket, to serve

· Heat the oil in a large, heavy-based frying pan. Toss the chicken breasts with plenty of pepper, add to the pan and cook, turning occasionally, over a high heat for 7–8 minutes or until golden and cooked through.

· Cut the ciabatta loaf halves into 4 pieces and cook them, cut side down, on a preheated hot griddle pan for 1–2 minutes or until lightly toasted.

· Mix together the chopped tomatoes, onion and parsley to make a salsa.

· Arrange the slices of chicken on the 4 ciabatta bases and top with salsa. Spread the ciabatta tops with mayonnaise and mustard, place on top and serve with rocket leaves.

---

2 **Hot Tomato, Caramelized Onion and Chicken Open Sandwich** Heat 4 tablespoons olive oil and cook 1 finely sliced red onion over a moderate heat, for 15 minutes or until soft and caramelized. Add 1 tablespoon soft brown sugar for the final 1 minute of cooking, then set aside. Make a salsa by mixing 1 finely chopped tomato with 3 tablespoons chopped coriander, season and set aside. Heat 1 tablespoon olive oil and cook 2 thinly sliced chicken breasts for 4–5 minutes or until golden. Slice 1 ciabatta loaf in half and spread with mayonnaise. Top with the hot chicken, onion and salsa. Add rocket leaves and serve.

---

3 **Chicken, Spinach, Tomato and Red Onion Gratin** Heat 4 tablespoons olive oil in a large, heavy-based frying pan and cook 4 diced chicken breasts, each about 150 g (5 oz), tossed with 1 tablespoon pepper over a moderate heat for 2 minutes. Add 4 roughly chopped tomatoes and 1 thinly sliced red onion and cook, stirring occasionally, for 10 minutes or until softened. Add 300 g (10 oz) fresh spinach leaves, stir and cook for 3 minutes or until the spinach has wilted. Transfer to a shallow, ovenproof gratin dish. Tear ¼ ciabatta loaf into small, rough pieces and scatter over the chicken. Scatter over 125 g (4 oz) grated medium mature Cheddar cheese and cook under a preheated moderate grill for 3–4 minutes or until golden and bubbling.

Chicken, Leek and Parsley Pies

Serves 4

375 g (12 oz) ready-rolled
   shortcrust pastry
1 egg, beaten
50 g (2 oz) butter
375 g (12 oz) chicken, diced
2 leeks, finely chopped
4 tablespoons chopped parsley
150 ml (¼ pint) white wine
150 ml (¼ pint) double cream
2 teaspoons Dijon mustard
salt and pepper

- Unroll the pastry and use a 15 cm (6 inch) saucer as a template to cut 4 circles. Place on a large baking sheet lined with baking parchment. (If you have time, cut leaves from the trimmings and place 4 on top of each circle.) Glaze with beaten egg and bake in a preheated oven, 200°C (400°F), Gas Mark 6, for 15 minutes or until golden and crisp.

- Meanwhile, heat the butter in a large, heavy-based frying pan and cook the chicken over a high heat for 10 minutes or until golden. Add the leeks and cook, stirring occasionally, for a further 5 minutes or until soft. Add the parsley and the wine. Stir, increase the heat and boil to reduce the wine by half.

- Add the cream and mustard and heat through, without boiling, for 1 minute until piping hot. Season generously and ladle the chicken mixture on to 4 warmed serving plates. Top each with a pastry circle and serve with vegetables.

 Creamy Chicken and Leeks with Cheesy Mash Heat 25 g (1 oz) butter in a large, heavy-based frying pan and cook 250 g (8 oz) thinly sliced chicken over a high heat for 5 minutes or until golden. Add 2 thinly sliced leeks and continue to cook over a high heat for 3 minutes or until softened. Add 200 ml (7 fl oz) crème fraîche to the pan with 1 teaspoon Dijon mustard and heat for a further 1 minute. Heat 600 g (1 lb 2 oz) ready-made cheesy mash and serve the chicken spooned over the mash.

Potato Cake Topped Chicken and Leek Pie Heat 25 g (1 oz) butter in a large, heavy-based frying pan and cook 350 g (11½ oz) chicken over a high heat for 10 minutes. Add 2 finely chopped leeks and continue to cook over a high heat for a further 5 minutes. Add 200 ml (7 fl oz) crème fraîche mixed with 2 teaspoons Dijon mustard and heat for 1 further minute until piping hot. Place 4 potato cakes on a foil-lined grill rack and cook under a preheated medium grill for 2–3 minutes or until piping hot. Serve the chicken and leek mixture ladled on to 4 warmed serving plates and place a warm potato cake on top of each.

Wholemeal Chicken Gougons with Lemon Mayonnaise

Serves 4

4 chicken breasts, each about
150 g (5 oz)

75 g (3 oz) plain flour

2 eggs, beaten

250 g (8 oz) wholemeal
breadcrumbs

2 teaspoons paprika

4 tablespoons chopped parsley

6 tablespoons vegetable oil

crudités: carrot sticks, sliced
peppers and sugar snap peas

For the lemon mayonnaise

150 ml (¼ pint) mayonnaise

finely grated rind and juice of
1 lemon

pepper

- Cut each chicken breast lengthways into 6 long slices and put them in a bowl with the flour. Toss well to coat, shaking to remove any excess. Put the beaten eggs in a large bowl. In a separate bowl mix together the wholemeal breadcrumbs, paprika and parsley well. Dip each chicken slice into the egg and then into the breadcrumbs.

- Heat the oil in a large, heavy-based frying pan and cook the chicken, in batches, over a moderately high heat, turning occasionally, for 4–5 minutes or until golden and crisp on the outside and cooked in the centre. Keep the cooked gougons warm while you cook the remainder.

- Meanwhile, make the lemon mayonnaise by mixing the mayonnaise with the lemon rind and juice in a small bowl and seasoning it well with pepper.

- Serve the warm gougons with the lemon mayonnaise and a selection of crudités.

---

10 **Pan-Fried Gougons with Lemon Mayo**

Cut 3 chicken breasts lengthways into 5 slices. In a large bowl mix together 4 tablespoons plain flour, ½ teaspoon pepper and ½ teaspoon chicken seasoning (optional). Lightly coat the chicken in the flour. Heat 3 tablespoons vegetable oil in a large frying pan and cook the chicken, turning frequently, for 7–8 minutes or until golden and cooked through. Meanwhile, mix 150 ml (¼ pint) mayonnaise with the grated rind and juice of 1 lemon and season well. Serve the hot chicken dipped in the lemon mayonnaise.

30 **Oven-Baked Chicken Parmesan Gougons with Roasted Peppers**

Preheat the oven to 200°C (400°F), Gas Mark 6. Cut 2 different coloured peppers into chunks and toss with 1 tablespoon olive oil. Place in a large roasting tin and roast in the oven while it is heating up. Meanwhile, cut 4 chicken breasts, each about 150 g (5 oz), into 4 thick slices. Mix together 125 g (4 oz) wholemeal breadcrumbs and 25 g (1 oz) freshly grated Parmesan cheese. Press the chicken firmly into the breadcrumbs to coat and

transfer to the roasting tin with the peppers. Cook for 20 minutes or until cooked through. Garnish sprinkled with 2 tablespoons chopped parsley and serve with mayonnaise blended with a little paprika to flavour, if liked.

30 Chicken Pesto Meatballs in Tomato Sauce with Pasta

Serves 4

125 g (4 oz) chicken mince
4 tablespoons pesto
4 tablespoons chopped basil
2 tablespoons olive oil
1 onion, roughly chopped
2 × 400 g (13 oz) cans chopped tomatoes
4 tablespoons tomato purée
salt and pepper
fresh pasta, to serve (optional)

- Put the mince in a mixing bowl with the pesto and basil and mash together with a fork to blend the pesto and herbs into the mince. Shape the mince into 24–30 small balls.

- Heat 1 tablespoon of the oil in a large, heavy-based frying pan and cook the chicken balls over a high heat, shaking the pan occasionally to turn the meatballs, for 15 minutes or until golden brown and cooked through.

- Meanwhile, heat the remaining oil in a separate frying pan and cook the onion over a moderately high heat for 3–4 minutes, stirring until softened. Add the chopped tomatoes and tomato purée and season generously with salt and pepper. Bring to the boil, then reduce the heat and simmer, uncovered, for 5 minutes or until the sauce has reduced and thickened slightly.

- Stir the meatballs into the tomato sauce and serve with fresh pasta shapes, if liked.

 Chicken Burgers with Pesto Dressing

Shape 375 g (12 oz) chicken mince into 4 patty shapes. Heat 1 tablespoon olive oil in a large, heavy-based frying pan and cook the burgers for 3–4 minutes on each side. Season generously with pepper and serve in a wholemeal bun with 1 teaspoon pesto spread over each one and a thick slice of tomato on top.

 Chicken Meatballs with Pesto Sauce

Shape 500 g (1 lb) chicken mince into 20 balls. Heat 1 tablespoon olive oil in a large, heavy-based frying pan and cook the chicken balls over a high heat for 15 minutes, shaking the pan occasionally to turn the balls until golden and cooked through. Add 4 tablespoons pesto sauce to the pan, shaking the pan to coat the meatballs in the pesto. Serve on fresh cooked pasta with Parmesan shavings, if liked.

CHI-FAMI-MUB

30 Butter and Lemon Roasted Chicken Thighs

Serves 4

8 boneless, skinless chicken
  thighs
finely grated rind and juice of
  1 lemon
3 tablespoons chopped parsley
50 g (2 oz) butter
pepper

- Put the chicken thighs in a large mixing bowl with the lemon rind and juice, parsley and plenty of pepper and mix well to coat the chicken. Roll each of the coated thighs back into shape and secure with a cocktail stick.

- Put the chicken thighs in a roasting tin, pouring any remaining juices over them, and top each with a small knob of butter. Cook in a preheated oven, 200°C (400°F), Gas Mark 6, for 20–25 minutes or until golden and cooked through. Serve with seasonal vegetables.

 1 **Lemon and Butter Pilaff**

Place 500 g (1 lb) mini-breast fillets into a bowl with the finely grated rind and juice of 1 lemon and 3 tablespoons chopped parsley. Season generously with salt and pepper. Heat 50 g (2 oz) butter in a large frying pan and cook the fillets over a high heat for 6–7 minutes, turning frequently until golden and cooked through. Toss in 2 x 250 g (8 oz) packets express flavoured rice of your choice and cook for a further 2 minutes. Serve immediately.

 2 **Pan-Fried Thighs with Lemon and Butter** Open out 8 boneless, skinless chicken thighs and cut in half along each width. Place the chicken pieces in a large mixing bowl with the rind and juice of 1 lemon and 3 tablespoons chopped parsley. Season with salt and pepper and miz well. Heat 50 g (2 oz) butter in a large, heavy-based frying pan and cook the chicken, turning frequently, for 15 minutes or until golden and cooked through. Serve with instant mashed potato or rice.

Tarragon Chicken Burgers with Spicy Salsa

Serves 4

450 g (14½ oz) chicken breast

50 g (2 oz) fresh white breadcrumbs

6 tablespoons chopped tarragon

1 tablespoon wholegrain mustard

1 tablespoon olive oil

4 wholemeal buns, split

4 slices of Brie

4 tablespoons ready-made spicy salsa

- Put the chicken breasts in a food processor or blender and process until smooth. Add the breadcrumbs, tarragon and mustard and process again. Shape the mixture into 4 balls and flatten them into 4 patties with lightly oiled hands.

- Heat the oil in large, heavy-based griddle pan or frying pan and cook the burgers, turning once, over a moderately high heat for 8–10 minutes or until golden and cooked through.

- Split the buns and serve the burgers in the buns with slices of Brie and a spoonful of spicy tomato salsa.

1 Hot Tarragon Chicken Rolls

Cut 3 chicken breasts, each about 125 g (4 oz), into 4 thin slices widthways and put them in a bowl with 1 tablespoon olive oil and 2 tablespoons chopped tarragon. Heat 1 tablespoon olive oil in a large, heavy-based frying pan and cook the chicken slices in a single layer, turning once, over a high heat for 5 minutes or until golden and cooked through. Serve piled into 4 wholemeal rolls and top while still warm with a slice of Emmenthal cheese and a spoonful of spicy tomato salsa, if liked.

3 Chilli and Coriander Chicken Burgers with Mango and Tomato Salsa

Put 375 g (12 oz) chicken breast in a food processor or blender and process until smooth. Add 50 g (2 oz) fresh white breadcrumbs, ½ finely chopped small chilli and 3 tablespoons chopped fresh coriander. Process again to blend. Use lightly oiled hands to shape the mixture into 4 balls and flatten them into 4 patty shapes. Heat 1 tablespoon olive oil in a pan and cook the burgers, turning once, over a moderately high heat for 8–10 minutes or until golden and cooked through. Make a salsa. Finely chop ½ ripe mango and place in a bowl with 4 finely chopped spring onions, 3 tablespoons chopped fresh coriander and ½ finely chopped small chilli. Mix well, season with pepper and serve spooned on to the burgers in 4 wholemeal buns with some dressed rocket on top.

Lentil and Chicken Stew

Serves 4

1 tablespoon olive oil

2 chicken breasts, each about
150 g (5 oz), thinly sliced

3 celery sticks, roughly chopped

4 roughly chopped tomatoes

250 g (8 oz) ready-cooked
Puy lentils

400 g (13 oz) can chopped
tomatoes

1 chicken stock cube, crumbled

2 tablespoons chopped parsley

- Heat the oil in a medium-sized, heavy-based frying pan and cook the chicken and celery for 5 minutes. Add the tomatoes and stir for 1 minute.

- Add the lentils, tomatoes and stock cube together with 150 ml (¼ pint) boiling water. Bring to the boil and keep at a boil for 2 minutes, stirring occasionally.

- Stir in the chopped parsley and serve ladled into serving bowls with crusty bread, if liked, to mop up the juices.

2 Chicken and Paprika Lentil Stew

Heat 1 tablespoon oil in a large, heavy-based saucepan and cook 1 chopped onion, 2 thinly sliced chicken breasts, each about 150 g (5 oz), for 5 minutes. Add 1 teaspoon smoked paprika and 6 chopped tomatoes and cook for 1 minute over a high heat. Add 250 g (8 oz) ready-cooked Puy lentils and 600 ml (1 pint) rich chicken stock. Bring to the boil and cook, uncovered, for 10–12 minutes or until the stew is rich and the stock has reduced slightly. Serve ladled into warmed serving bowls, with warm crusty bread to mop up the juices.

3 Thick Red Lentil and Chicken Stew

Heat 1 tablespoon olive oil and cook 2 (150 g (5 oz)) thinly sliced chicken breasts, 1 large thinly sliced onion and 4 celery sticks over a moderately high heat for 5 minutes. Add 4 roughly chopped tomatoes, 250 g (8 oz) red lentils, 400 g (13 oz) can chopped tomatoes and 600 ml (1 pint) chicken stock. Bring to the boil, reduce the heat, cover and simmer, stirring occasionally, for 20 minutes or until the lentils are soft and tender. Season with salt and pepper and stir in 6 tablespoons chopped parsley. Serve with warm crusty bread.

Pan-Fried Chicken with Tomato Basil Salsa and Goats' Cheese

Serves 4

4 tablespoons olive oil
4 chicken breasts, each about 125 g (4 oz)
2 ripe plum tomatoes, finely chopped
4 tablespoons chopped basil leaves
1 small red onion, finely chopped
1 tablespoon balsamic vinegar
4 thick slices of rinded goats' cheese
salt and pepper

To serve
salad
crusty bread

- Heat 2 tablespoons olive oil in a large, heavy-based frying pan. Slice the chicken breasts in half widthways, almost all the way through, opening the chicken out on its hinge to form a 'butterfly'. Season all over with a little salt and pepper. Cook the chicken over a moderately high heat for 5 minutes on each side or until golden and cooked through.

- Meanwhile, make a salsa. Mix together plum tomatoes, basil and red onion, the remaining oil and the balsamic vinegar. Season to taste with salt and pepper.

- Put a slice of goats' cheese on each of the chicken breasts, cover the pan with a lid and cook for a further 1–2 minutes over a gentle heat or until the cheese melts slightly. Serve the hot chicken on warmed serving plates with the salsa spooned over and with a simple salad and crusty bread, if liked.

---

10 Chicken, Goats' Cheese and Sun-Blush Tomato Toastie

Thinly slice 2 chicken breasts, each about 150 g (5 oz). Heat 2 tablespoons olive oil in a large frying pan and cook the chicken over a high heat for 8 minutes or until golden and cooked through. Meanwhile, toss 75 g (3 oz) sun-blush tomatoes with 2 tablespoons chopped basil leaves. Lightly toast 4 thick slices of wholemeal bread. Arrange the hot chicken on the toast and top with a slice of goats' cheese. Allow the cheese to melt a little before topping with the basil and tomato mixture.

---

30 Chicken, Plum Tomato, Basil and Goats' Cheese Bake

Heat 2 tablespoons olive oil in a large, heavy-based frying pan and cook 4 chicken breasts, each about 150 g (5 oz), over a high heat for 2 minutes on each side until golden. Transfer to a small, shallow gratin dish. Slice 4 large plum tomatoes and place in the dish with the chicken, then scatter over 4 tablespoons chopped basil leaves. Slice 250 g (8 oz) rinded goats' cheese and place over the top. Season generously with pepper, drizzle with 2 tablespoons olive oil and bake in a preheated oven, 200°C (400°F), Gas Mark 6, for 15–20 minutes or until the cheese is golden and the chicken cooked through. Serve with a simple salad and crusty bread.

CHI-FAMI-DOX

3⦿ Fajitas

Serves 4

3 tablespoons olive oil

1 red, 1 green and 1 orange pepper, cored, deseeded and cut into chunks

375 g (12 oz) chicken breasts, diced

2 red onions, cut into thin wedges

1 courgette, cut into chunks

1 tablespoon Cajun spice

1 tablespoon chopped thyme leaves

8 soft flour tortilla wraps

1 avocado, peeled, stoned and roughly chopped

finely grated rind and juice of ½ lime

salt and pepper

To serve

½ lime cut into wedges

soured cream

- Heat the oil in a large, heavy-based frying pan and cook the peppers, chicken and onions over a high heat, stirring continually, for 10 minutes or until golden in places. Add the courgette and the Cajun spice, toss and stir-fry for a further 10 minutes or until the chicken is cooked and the vegetables are softened and lightly charred in places. Stir in the thyme leaves.

- Warm the flour tortillas in a warm oven or microwave. Meanwhile, to make the guacamole, put the avocado in a bowl and mash well with a fork until smooth but still textured. Season generously with salt and pepper, add the lime rind and juice and stir well to combine.

- Serve the warm tortillas filled with spoonfuls of the chicken mixture, soured cream and guacamole, and either rolled or folded, and accompanied by a simple salad, if liked.

1⦿ Spicy Chicken and Tomato Fajita with Sliced Avocado Heat 2 tablespoons olive oil in a large, heavy-based frying pan and cook 375 g (12 oz) diced chicken over a high heat for 7 minutes. Add 2 teaspoons Cajun spice and 10 halved cherry tomatoes and stir-fry for 2 minutes before removing from the heat and adding a sliced avocado. Serve in warmed tortilla wraps.

2⦿ Chicken, Pepper and Warm Avocado Wraps with Paprika Heat 2 tablespoons olive oil in a large, heavy-based frying pan and cook 375 g (12 oz) diced chicken and 1 large sliced red onion over a high heat for 7–8 minutes or until beginning to turn golden. Add 1 large sliced red and 1 orange pepper and continue to cook over a high heat for 4 minutes. Add 2 tablespoons chopped thyme leaves and 2 teaspoons paprika and continue to cook for 2 minutes. Slice 1 ripe avocado and toss through the mixture. Warm 4 flour tortillas in a low oven or microwave and spoon the filling between them. Fold to eat, with a simple watercress salad dressed with lime juice.

30 Sticky Soy-Glazed Drumsticks

Serves 4

8 chicken drumsticks
2 tablespoons clear honey
2 tablespoons olive oil
2 tablespoons dark soy sauce
1 teaspoon tomato purée
1 tablespoon Dijon mustard
chopped parsley, to garnish

- Put the drumsticks on a board and make 4 deep slashes in each ome along the thick part of the meat, cutting down to the bone on both sides.

- In a large bowl mix together the honey, oil, soy sauce, tomato purée and mustard. Toss the drumsticks in the glaze, turning to cover the meat well.

- Transfer the drumsticks to a roasting tin and roast in the top of a preheated oven, 220°C (425°F), Gas Mark 7, for 20–25 minutes or until the chicken is cooked through. Garnish with parsley and serve with boiled rice and a salad, if liked.

 10 Soy-Glazed Stir-Fry

Heat 2 tablespoons sunflower oil in a large wok or frying pan and cook 250 g (8 oz) thinly sliced chicken breast over a high heat for 2 minutes. Add 175 g (6 oz) sugar snap peas, 175 g (6 oz) mangetout and 1 head shredded pak choi. Stir-fry over a high heat for a further 5 minutes, stirring almost continually. Mix together 2 tablespoons dark soy sauce and 2 tablespoons clear honey, pour into the stir-fry and toss and cook for 1 minute more before serving.

 20 Sticky Chilli Soy-Glazed

Chicken Breasts Mix together the honey, oil, soy sauce, tomato purée and mustard as above to make the glaze and add 1 finely chopped small red chilli. Coat 4 chicken breasts, each about 125 g (4 oz), in the glaze. Heat 1 tablespoon olive oil in a large, heavy-based frying pan and cook the chicken over a moderately high heat for 15 minutes, turning it regularly and reducing the heat a little if the glaze begins to catch on the base of the pan. Slice the cooked chicken and serve fanned on a plate, with boiled rice and salad.

2 Simple Mango and Coconut Curry with Coriander

Serves 4

1 tablespoon vegetable oil

1 large onion, chopped

500 g (1 lb) diced chicken meat

1 large, ripe mango, peeled, stoned and cut into chunks

1 teaspoon ground coriander

1 teaspoon ground cumin

2 tablespoons korma curry paste

400 ml (14 fl oz) coconut milk

300 ml (½ pint) rich chicken stock

6 tablespoons chopped fresh coriander

1 tablespoon cornflour

- Heat the oil in a large, heavy-based frying pan or wok and cook the onion and chicken over a high heat for 5 minutes or until golden and beginning to soften.

- Add the chopped mango, spices and curry paste and stir for a few seconds before adding the coconut milk and stock. Bring to the boil, then reduce the heat and simmer, uncovered and stirring occasionally, for 10–12 minutes, then add the fresh coriander.

- Blend the cornflour with 2 tablespoons water, pour into the hot curry and stir well to thicken. Serve with rice and poppadoms.

1 Pulpy Mango and Chicken Curry

Heat 1 tablespoon oil in a large, heavy-based frying pan and cook 375 g (12 oz) diced chicken for 2 minutes. Add 2 tablespoons curry paste, 300 ml (½ pint) can mango pulp and 400 ml (14 fl oz) can coconut milk. Bring to the boil, reduce the heat and simmer for 7 minutes. Add 250 g (8 oz) frozen peas for the final 3 minutes of cooking. Serve with toasted naan bread fingers.

3 Caribbean-Style Chicken, Mango and Plantain Curry

Heat 2 tablespoons oil in a large, heavy-based frying pan or wok and cook 500 g (1 lb) diced chicken meat with 1 large chopped onion for 5 minutes. Stone 1 large mango, chop the flesh and add to the pan with 250 g (8 oz) chopped or sliced plantain. Add 1 teaspoon ground coriander, 1 teaspoon ground cumin and 3 tablespoons curry paste and cook, stirring, for 1 minute. Add 2 × 400 ml (14 fl oz) cans coconut milk. Bring to the boil, reduce the heat, cover and simmer for 20 minutes. Add 5 tablespoons chopped fresh coriander and stir through. Serve with rice mixed with kidney beans.

30 Chicken Chilli with Potato Wedges and Guacamole

Serves 4

850 g (1¾ lb) ready-prepared
  potato wedges
3 tablespoons oil
500 g (1 lb) chicken mince
1 tablespoon mild chilli powder
2 teaspoons ground cumin
2 teaspoons ground coriander
400 g (13 oz) can chopped
  tomatoes
150 ml (¼ pint) rich chicken stock
400 g (13 oz) can red kidney
  beans, rinsed and drained
1 tablespoon chopped coriander

For the guacamole

1 ripe avocado
1 tablespoon lemon juice
pinch of chilli powder

- Toss the potato wedges in 2 tablespoons of the oil and place in a single layer on a baking sheet and roast in a preheated oven, 220°C (425°F), Gas Mark 7, for 20–25 minutes or until lightly golden and cooked.

- Meanwhile, heat the remaining oil oil in a large, heavy-based frying pan and cook the chicken mince over a high heat, stirring frequently, for 10 minutes or until the chicken is golden in places. Add the chilli, cumin and coriander and cook for 2 minutes. Add the tomatoes and chicken stock and bring to the boil. Reduce the heat, simmer for 10 minutes and add the kidney beans. Cook for a further 5 minutes.

- Meanwhile, mash the avocado in a bowl with the lemon juice and stir in the chilli powder. Serve the chicken with the potato wedges lightly stirred through on warmed serving plates, with spoonfuls of chunky guacamole and chopped coriander scattered over the top.

 Simple Chunky Chicken Chilli

with Guacamole Dice 3 cooked chicken breasts, each about 125 g (4 oz), and place in a pan with 400 g (13 oz) jar chilli sauce, 275 g (9 oz) jar roasted red peppers, drained and roughly chopped, and 400 g (13 oz) can kidney beans, rinsed and drained. Bring to the boil, reduce the heat and simmer for 7–8 minutes or until piping hot. Serve with ready-made guacamole and crusty bread.

 Chicken Chilli with Peppers

Heat 2 tablespoons oil in a large, heavy-based frying pan and cook 1 large chopped onion, 1 chopped red and 1 chopped orange pepper with 500 g (1 lb) chicken mince over a high heat for 10 minutes or until golden. Add 1 tablespoon mild chilli powder and 400 g (13 oz) jar chilli sauce. Bring to the boil, stirring, then reduce the heat and simmer for 5 minutes before serving with chopped fresh coriander to garnish. Serve with express rice or naan bread.

QuickCook
Food for Friends

Recipes listed by cooking time

30 Chicken Parmigiana

Serves 4

2 chicken breasts, each about 175 g (6 oz), halved lengthways

2 eggs, beaten

75 g (3 oz) breadcrumbs

75 g (3 oz) freshly grated Parmesan cheese

1 tablespoon olive oil

2 garlic cloves, crushed

350 g (11½ oz) ready-made passata

1 teaspoon caster sugar

1 teaspoon dried oregano

150 g (5 oz) mozzarella cheese, drained

- Put the chicken breasts between 2 sheets of clingfilm and beat with a rolling pin until they are 1 cm (½ inch) thick. Dip the chicken in the egg and then in the breadcrumbs mixed with half the Parmesan. Set aside on a plate in the refrigerator.

- Meanwhile, heat the oil in a large, heavy-based frying pan and cook the garlic for a few seconds. Add the passata, sugar and oregano. Simmer for 5–8 minutes until thick and pulpy.

- Cook the chicken under a preheated hot grill for 5 minutes on each side until pale golden. Pour the tomato sauce into a shallow, ovenproof gratin dish and top with the chicken. Scatter over the mozzarella and remaining Parmesan and grill for 3–4 minutes until the cheese has melted and the sauce is bubbling. Serve with salad or vegetables, if liked.

---

10 Cherry Tomato and Garlic Chicken

Pan-Fry Heat 2 tablespoons olive oil in a large, heavy-based frying pan and cook 250 g (8 oz) diced chicken meat over a high heat for 3 minutes. Add 250 g (8 oz) whole cherry tomatoes and stir-fry for a further 5 minutes. Add 1 teaspoon minced garlic, 100 g (3½ oz) pitted black olives and 150 ml (¼ pint) passata and cook over a high heat for a further 1 minute until the passata is piping hot. Serve in warmed serving bowls with plenty of freshly grated Parmesan cheese and warm crusty bread.

20 Chicken and Tomato Pasta

Gratin Cook 250 g (8 oz) pasta shapes in a large saucepan of lightly salted boiling water for 8–10 minutes or until tender. Meanwhile, heat 3 tablespoons olive oil in a large, heavy-based frying pan and cook 2 thinly sliced chicken breasts, each about 150 g (5 oz), over a high heat for 5 minutes or until golden. Add a crushed garlic clove and 700 g (1 lb 7 oz) ready-made passata and 1 teaspoon dried oregano and bring to the boil. Drain the pasta and stir with the chicken and tomato sauce. Transfer to a large, shallow ovenproof dish and scatter over 75 g (3 oz) fresh breadcrumbs mixed with 75 g (3 oz) freshly grated Parmesan cheese. PLace under a preheated hot grill for 3–4 minutes until golden and bubbling.

30 Greek-Style Chicken Thighs with Olives and Green Beans

Serves 4

2 tablespoons olive oil

4 chicken thighs

1 large red onion, sliced

250 g (8 oz) cherry tomatoes, halved

400 g (13 oz) can chopped tomatoes with garlic and herbs

4 tablespoons sun-dried tomato paste

125 g (4 oz) kalamata olives, drained

150 ml (¼ pint) red wine

175 g (6 oz) trimmed green beans

50 g (2 oz) crumbled feta cheese, to serve

- Heat the oil in large, heavy-based frying pan and cook the chicken thighs and red onion over a high heat for 5 minutes, turning once, until golden.

- Add the cherry tomatoes and stir-fry for 2 minutes, then add the chopped tomatoes and tomato paste and bring to the boil. Reduce the heat, cover and simmer for 15 minutes. Add the wine and the beans and stir again. Re-cover the pan and cook for 5 minutes more until the beans are just tender and the chicken is cooked through.

- Serve ladled into warmed bowls and scattered with the crumbled feta. Accompany with warm continental crusty bread to mop up the juices, if liked.

10 Greek Salad with Mixed Herb Dressing

Chop ½ cucumber into chunks and put in a salad bowl with 250 g (8 oz) sliced cooked chicken, 250 g (8 oz) halved baby cherry tomatoes and 125 g (4 oz) kalamata olives. Toss together well. Make a dressing by whisking together 4 tablespoons olive oil, 2 tablespoons red wine vinegar, 1 teaspoon Dijon mustard and ½ teaspoon dried mixed herbs. Pour over the salad ingredients and toss well to coat.

20 Greek-Style Mixed Olive, Chicken and Tomato Pizza

Put a ready-made pizza base, 23 cm (9 inches) across, on a baking sheet and spread with 3 tablespoons sun-dried tomato paste. Scatter over 125 g (4 oz) sliced cooked chicken, 125 g (4 oz) halved cherry tomatoes and 125 g (4 oz) mixed assorted olives, including kalamata black olives. Sprinkle over 125 g (4 oz) grated mozzarella cheese and scatter over 50 g (2 oz) finely crumbled feta cheese. Bake in the top of a preheated oven, 220°C (425°F), Gas Mark 7, for 10–12 minutes or until golden and bubbling. Serve drizzled with olive oil.

20 Gingered Chicken, Seed and Vegetable Rice

Serves 4

250 g (8 oz) easy-cook
   brown rice
2 tablespoons olive oil
300 g (10 oz) diced chicken
1 tablespoon ginger paste
1 onion, thinly sliced
4 tablespoons sunflower seeds
3 tablespoons pumpkin seeds
1 tablespoon black mustard seeds
1 large courgette, grated
1 large carrot, grated
175 g (6 oz) petit pois

- Cook the rice in a large saucepan of lightly salted boiling water for 15 minutes or until tender.

- Meanwhile, put 1 tablespoon of the oil in a large mixing bowl with the chicken and ginger paste and mix well to lightly coat the chicken. Add the chicken and onion to a large, heavy-based frying pan and cook, stirring occasionally, for 10 minutes or until golden in places and cooked through.

- Meanwhile, in a separate pan heat the remaining oil and cook the seeds for 1 minute to brown a little. Add the courgette and carrot and stir-fry for 3 minutes until softened, then add the petit pois and stir-fry for a further 2–3 minutes until piping hot.

- Drain the rice and add to the pan with the chicken. Toss well then add the hot seeds, courgette, carrot and petit pois and toss again. Serve hot in warmed serving bowls.

---

1 Chicken Couscous
Make 110 g (3½ oz) lemon- and coriander-flavoured couscous according to the instructions on the packet and set aside to swell. Meanwhile, heat a large, heavy-based frying pan and toss 375 g (12 oz) diced chicken with 1 tablespoon ginger paste and 1 tablespoon olive oil. Cook in the hot pan, stirring occasionally, for 8 minutes or until golden and cooked through. Toss the chicken with the couscous and 4 tablespoons chopped fresh coriander and serve immediately.

3 Gingered Chicken Pilaff with Roasted Vegetables Roughly chop 2 large courgettes and 2 large carrots and cut 2 red onions into thin wedges. Place them in a roasting tin with 4 tablespoons olive oil and toss in the oil to coat. Roast in a preheated oven, 200°C (400°F), Gas Mark 6, for 20 minutes until tender and lightly charred in places. Meanwhile, bring a large pan of lightly salted water to the boil and cook 250 g (8 oz) rice for 15 minutes or until tender, then drain. Meanwhile, toss 375 g

(12 oz) diced chicken with 1 tablespoon olive oil and 1 tablespoon ginger paste and cook in a large, heavy-based preheated frying pan for 10 minutes or until cooked through and golden. Toss the rice, roasted vegetables and chicken together and mix with 4 tablespoons chopped fresh coriander before serving.

Grilled Gazpacho Chicken Salad

Serves 4

6 tablespoons olive oil

4 tablespoons finely chopped basil

3 chicken breasts, each about 150 g (5 oz)

375 g (12 oz) piquante peppers, (165 g/5½ oz drained)

1 bunch of spring onions, roughly chopped

½ cucumber, roughly chopped

250 g (8 oz) cherry plum tomatoes, halved

4 tablespoons chopped flat leaf parsley

- Put 2 tablespoons of the oil in a shallow bowl with 3 tablespoons of the basil. Brush the mixture over the chicken breasts. Place the chicken on a foil-lined grill rack and cook under a preheated hot grill for 5–6 minutes on each side or until golden and cooked through.

- Meanwhile, put the piquante peppers in a large salad bowl with the spring onions, cucumber, cherry tomatoes and parsley and toss together. Add the remaining oil and basil and toss again.

- Cut the hot chicken into thin slices and toss into the salad. Serve with warm crusty bread, if liked.

1️⃣ Gazpacho Soup with Chicken Salsa

Put 4 quartered tomatoes in a food processor or blender with 3 drained piquante peppers, 4 chopped spring onions, ¼ roughly chopped cucumber and process until thick and smooth. Add 400 g (13 oz) can chopped tomatoes and blend again. Meanwhile, chop 1 cooked chicken breast, about 125 g (4 oz), into small pieces and mix with 1 tablespoon chopped parsley. Ladle the cold soup into 4 serving bowls and top each serving with a spoonful of chicken salsa.

3️⃣ Gazpacho Chicken Bake with Cucumber and Piquante Salsa

Toss 4 chicken breasts, each about 125 g (4 oz), in 2 tablespoons olive oil, 2 tablespoons chopped basil and plenty of pepper. Transfer to a large roasting tin, add 375 g (12 oz) halved cherry tomatoes and drizzle with 2 tablespoons olive oil. Season with ½ teaspoon salt flakes and pepper. Top with 125 g (4 oz) fresh white breadcrumbs tossed with 4 tablespoons chopped parsley and 4 tablespoons freshly grated Parmesan cheese. Roast in a preheated oven, 220 °C (425 °F), Gas Mark 7, for 20 minutes until the chicken is golden and the cherry tomatoes are soft. Meanwhile, make a salsa of ¼ finely chopped cucumber, 1 small finely chopped red chilli, 4 finely chopped piquante peppers and 3 tablespoons chopped parsley. Serve the hot gazpacho chicken bake with spoonfuls of salsa on top.

# Simple Warm Chicken Liver Pâté

Serves 4

25 g (1 oz) butter
375 g (12 oz) chicken livers,
 well drained
1 onion, roughly chopped
1 tablespoon sherry
1 tablespoon chopped thyme
 leaves (optional)
pepper

- Heat the butter in a large, heavy-based frying pan and cook the chicken livers and onion over a high heat for 7–8 minutes or until softened and golden. Add the sherry and shake the pan to mix.

- Put the chicken and onion in a food processor or blender and process until creamy and smooth. Season generously with pepper and stir through 1 tablespoon chopped thyme leaves, if liked.

- Serve spooned on to serving plates with warm toast, salad and ready-made onion chutney.

2 Chicken Liver Salad with Walnuts

Heat 2 tablespoons olive oil in a large, heavy-based frying pan and cook 1 sliced red onion and 375 g (12 oz) well-drained chicken livers over a high heat for 8–10 minutes or until golden and soft. Add 125 g (4 oz) walnut pieces and cook for a further 2 minutes. Put 150 g (5 oz) salad leaves in a salad bowl with 125 g (4 oz) halved baby plum tomatoes and add the warm chicken livers, onion and walnuts. In a small jug mix together 3 tablespoons olive oil and 2 tablespoons balsamic vinegar and whisk well. Pour over the salad and toss. Serve immediately.

3 Warm Chicken Liver Terrine

with Pistachios Cook 500 g (1 lb) well-drained chicken livers, 6 rashers of smoked, chopped back bacon and 1 chopped onion in a large, heavy-based frying pan over a high heat for 8–10 minutes or until golden and soft. Add 2 tablespoons brandy, stir and remove from the heat. Transfer the mixture to a food processor or blender and process until smooth. Turn into a mixing bowl, add 125 g (4 oz) roughly chopped pistachios and mix well. Line a 500 g (1 lb) loaf tin with clingfilm, spoon the warm mixture into the tin and press down well. Turn the warm terrine on to a serving plate and garnish with thyme leaves. Serve in slices with warm toasted rolls and a simple salad.

Sesame and Thyme Skewers with Spiced Chickpea Mash

Serves 4

3 chicken breasts, each about 150 g (5 oz), cut into small chunks

3 tablespoons sesame oil

1 tablespoon chopped thyme leaves

2 tablespoons sesame seeds

2 tablespoons olive oil

1 onion, chopped

1 small red chilli, chopped

2 thyme sprigs, plus extra to garnish (optional)

2 × 400 g (13 oz) cans chickpeas, rinsed and drained

6 tablespoons hot chicken stock

salt and pepper

- Put the chicken pieces in a bowl with the sesame oil, thyme leaves and sesame seeds and toss to coat. Thread the chicken evenly on to 8 skewers and arrange on a foil-lined grill rack. Place under a preheated grill, turning frequently, for 10 minutes or until golden and cooked through.

- Meanwhile, heat the oil in a heavy-based frying pan and cook the onion, chilli and thyme sprigs over a moderately high heat for 3–4 minutes or until the onion is soft and becoming golden. Add the chickpeas. Heat, stirring, for 1 minute, then add the stock, cover the pan with a lid, bring to the boil and cook for 3 minutes until piping hot. Season well. Transfer to a food processor or blender and process until almost smooth but still holding some texture.

- Spoon the chickpea purée on to serving plates and top each with a chicken skewer. Garnish with thyme sprigs, if liked.

 Thyme and Sesame Stir-Fry with Chickpeas Heat 1 tablespoon sesame oil in a large, heavy-based frying pan and cook 375 g (12 oz) diced chicken for 3–4 minutes over a high heat. Add ½ teaspoon dried thyme leaves and 2 tablespoons sesame seeds and continue to stir-fry for 2 minutes. Add 1 sliced red chilli and 2 × 400 g (13 oz) cans chickpeas. Cook, stirring, for a further 2 minutes until piping hot. Serve sprinkled with 4 tablespoons chopped fresh coriander leaves.

Minted Yogurt Chicken Skewers with Warm Chickpea Salad Cut 4 chicken breasts into pieces and put them in a bowl with a mixture of 2 teaspoons ground coriander, 1 teaspoon ground cumin, 150 g (10 oz) natural yogurt, the juice of ½ lemon, 1 tablespoon olive oil, 1 crushed garlic clove and 2 tablespoons chopped mint leaves. Mix well to coat. Thread the chicken evenly on to 8 bamboo or metal skewers. Place them on a foil-lined grill rack and cook under a preheated moderate grill, turning regularly, for 15 minutes. Meanwhile, thinly slice 1 onion. Heat 2 tablespoons olive oil and cook the onion over a moderately high heat with 1 teaspoon cumin seeds for 3–4 minutes until beginning to soften. Add 1 small chopped red chilli and continue to cook for a further 1 minute before adding 2 × 400 g (13 oz) cans drained chickpeas. Add 6 tablespoons chicken stock or water, cover and simmer for 2–3 minutes until piping hot. Sprinkle with 5 tablespoons chopped fresh coriander and serve spooned on to warm serving plates with the minted kebabs on top.

30 Chicken, Spinach, Onion Chutney and Goats' Cheese Tarts

Serves 4

375 g (12 oz) ready-rolled puff
  pastry, cut into 4 equal
  rectangles
2 tablespoons olive oil
250 g (8 oz) chicken, diced
200 g (7 oz) spinach leaves
½ teaspoon ground nutmeg
1 teaspoon mustard seeds
8 tablespoons ready-made red or
  white onion chutney
8 thick slices of rinded goats'
  cheese
salt and pepper

- Put the 4 pastry sheets on a large baking sheet and prick all over with a fork.

- Heat the oil in a large, heavy-based frying pan and cook the chicken over a high heat for 3 minutes. Add the spinach leaves, toss and cook for 1 minute until wilted. Remove from the heat, add the nutmeg and mustard seeds and season with a little salt and pepper, tossing well to coat.

- Drain the mixture if necessary, then spoon evenly on to the 4 sheets of pastry to within 2.5 cm (1 inch) of the edges. Spoon 2 tablespoons of onion chutney over the top of each and put the goats' cheese on top. Bake in a preheated oven, 220°C (425°F), Gas Mark 7, for 20 minutes until puffed and golden. Serve with a simple salad.

 Chicken, Spinach and Goats' Cheese Tarts Heat 1 tablespoon olive oil and 15 g (½ oz) butter in a large, heavy-based frying pan and cook 250 g (8 oz) diced chicken for 5 minutes. Add 100 g (3½ oz) spinach leaves and toss and stir for 2 minutes. Add ½ teaspoon ground nutmeg and season well. Chop 50 g (2 oz) rinded goats' cheese into small cubes and stir into the chicken and spinach. Spoon the mixture into 4 ready-made pastry cases and serve with salad.

 Chicken, Spinach and Goats' Cheese Pizza Put a ready-made pizza base, 23 cm (9 inches) across, on a baking sheet and cook under a preheated moderate grill for 2 minutes until warm. Meanwhile, heat 2 tablespoons olive oil in a large, heavy-based frying pan and cook 175 g (6 oz) diced chicken over a high heat for 3 minutes. Add 200 g (7 oz) spinach leaves and ½ teaspoon nutmeg, toss and cook for 1 minute until the spinach has wilted. Arrange over the top of the pizza base, spoon over 8 teaspoons onion chutney and then 6 slices of rinded goats' cheese. Replace under the grill, not too close to the element, and cook for 5–6 minutes until the top is warm, melted and golden.

Chicken and Fennel Risotto with Vermouth

Serves 4

3 tablespoons olive oil

50 g (2 oz) butter

1 onion, thinly sliced

1 fennel head, trimmed and thinly sliced

1 chicken breast, about 150 g (5 oz), finely sliced into small strips

1 teaspoon fennel seeds, roughly crushed

200 g (7 oz) easy-cook risotto rice

3 tablespoons vermouth

600 ml (1 pint) rich chicken stock

freshly grated Parmesan cheese, to serve

rocket, to garnish

- Heat the oil and butter in a large, heavy-based frying pan and cook the onion and fennel, stirring occasionally, over a moderately high heat for 5 minutes or until softened and golden in places. Add the chicken and fennel seeds and stir-fry for a further 2 minutes.

- Add the rice and vermouth to the pan. Increase the heat for a few seconds to burn off the alcohol, stirring continually, then add half the chicken stock. Cook, stirring occasionally, at a moderate heat until almost all the stock has been absorbed, then add the remaining stock and continue to cook in the same way for about 10–15 minutes, reducing the heat to a simmer until the rice is tender and cooked but still with a slight bite.

- Serve in warmed serving bowls with plenty of freshly grated Parmesan, a small handful of rocket on top and warm crusty bread, if liked.

 Fennel and Chicken Pilaff

Heat 2 tablespoons olive oil in a large, heavy-based frying pan and cook 1 roughly chopped trimmed fennel head with 250 g (8 oz) diced chicken meat over a high heat for 5 minutes or until softened and golden. Add 1 roughly chopped bunch of spring onions and ½ teaspoon fennel seeds and continue to cook for a further 1 minute. Add 250 g (8 oz) express rice and continue stir-frying for a further 2 minutes until piping hot. Serve with a rocket salad.

 Chicken, Bacon and Fennel Risotto with Roasted Butternut Squash

Roughly chop 500 g (1 lb) butternut squash, toss in 2 tablespoons olive oil and roast in a preheated oven, 200°C (400°F), Gas Mark 6, for 20 minutes until softened and lightly charred. Meanwhile, make the risotto as above, adding 4 rashers of finely chopped streaky bacon to the pan with the chicken and cooking for the same time. Once the risotto is cooked, fold in the butternut squash and serve with rocket.

1 Panzanella with Chicken

Serves 4

½ ciabatta loaf, torn into pieces
4 tablespoons olive oil
½ cucumber, roughly chopped
2 large tomatoes, roughly chopped
2 cooked chicken breasts, about
   250 g (8 oz) in total, torn into
   pieces
1 small red onion, roughly chopped
8 tablespoons ready-made
   French dressing
2 tablespoons chopped basil
salt and pepper

- Put the ciabatta pieces in a roasting tin and drizzle with the olive oil. Place under a preheated hot grill for 2–3 minutes until golden and warm.

- Meanwhile, put the cucumber, tomatoes, chicken, onion and dressing in a large mixing bowl. Add the chopped basil and mix well. Season with salt and black pepper.

- Add the warm ciabatta pieces to the bowl and toss well to coat in the dressing. Serve with extra French dressing, if liked.

2 Chicken, Tomato and Courgette

Bruschetta Heat 2 tablespoons olive oil in a large frying pan and cook 2 thinly sliced chicken breasts, each about 150 g (5 oz), over a high heat for 5 minutes. Add 1 finely chopped courgette and cook for a further 5 minutes before adding 2 roughly chopped tomatoes and 1 tablespoon chopped rosemary leaves. Cook over a high heat for 2–3 minutes until the tomatoes are soft yet still retain their shape. Meanwhile, cut ¼ ciabatta loaf into as wide slices as possible diagonally and lightly brush each with a little olive oil. Heat a griddle and cook the bread slices for 30 seconds on each side to lightly toast. Place on warmed serving plates and spoon over the warm chicken.

3 Courgette and Tomato Bake

Heat 4 tablespoons olive oil in a large frying pan and cook 375 g (12 oz) diced chicken meat over a high heat for 5 minutes. Add 1 large roughly chopped courgette and 1 roughly chopped red onion and cook for a further 5 minutes. Add 500 g (1 lb) ready-made tomato pasta sauce with herbs and heat for 1–2 minutes until hot. Transfer to a large, shallow ovenproof gratin dish and scatter over ¼ roughly torn ciabatta loaf. Drizzle with 1 tablespoon olive oil. Bake in a preheated oven, 200°C (400°F), Gas Mark 6, for 15 minutes until the top is pale golden and the sauce bubbling. Serve with a simple salad or green vegetables.

30 Lemon and Garlic Chicken Breasts with Rosemary Gravy

Serves 4

4 chicken breasts, each about
 150 g (5 oz) (with skin on)
1 lemon, sliced
4 rosemary sprigs
8 garlic cloves, peeled
2 tablespoons olive oil
salt and pepper
green beans and boiled potatoes,
 to serve

For the gravy

1 tablespoon olive oil
1 tablespoon chopped rosemary
 leaves
300 ml (½ pint) chicken stock
6 tablespoons white wine
2 teaspoons cornflour

- Make a large slit in the side of each chicken breast and insert 2 slices of lemon, 1 rosemary sprig and a halved garlic clove. Tie each chicken with with string around the centre, then put the chicken in a roasting tin, drizzle with olive oil and season generously with salt and pepper. Roast in a preheated oven, 220°C (425°F), Gas Mark 7, for 20–25 minutes or until golden and cooked through.

- Meanwhile, make the gravy. Heat the oil in a small saucepan and cook the rosemary leaves for 1 minute over a moderate heat. Pour in the stock and wine and bring to the boil. Continue to boil for 5 minutes to infuse the flavours and reduce a little. Blend the cornflour with 2 tablespoons water and add to the gravy, stirring continually to thicken. Pour over the roasted chicken pieces and serve with green beans and boiled potatoes.

10 Fusilli with Rosemary, Lemon and Garlic Chicken Cook 250 g (8 oz) fusilli in a large saucepan of lightly salted boiling water for 8–10 minutes or until tender. Meanwhile, heat 6 tablespoons garlic-infused olive oil in a large, heavy-based frying pan and cook 250 g (8 oz) diced chicken for 5 minutes over a high heat. Add 2 tablespoons chopped rosemary and cook for 2 minutes. Drain the pasta well and add to the pan with the chicken and rosemary. Add the grated rind and juice of 1 lemon. Toss well and serve hot.

20 Chicken, Lemon and Rosemary Risotto Heat 2 tablespoons olive oil in a large, heavy-based frying pan and cook 250 g (8 oz) diced chicken with 1 chopped garlic clove and 1 tablespoon chopped rosemary for 5 minutes over a high heat. Add 200 g (7 oz) easy-cook long grain rice to the pan with the finely grated rind and juice of 1 lemon and 600 ml (1 pint) chicken stock. Bring to the boil, cover and simmer, stirring, for 12–15 minutes or until the rice is tender and cooked. Serve spooned into warmed serving bowls with a rocket salad.

30 Smoked Chicken, Tomato and Salami Calzone

Serves 4

200 g (7 oz) pizza base mix

125 g (4 oz) smoked chicken, chopped

125 g (4 oz) cherry tomatoes, quartered

75 g (3 oz) Milano salami, roughly chopped

1 tablespoon chopped parsley

4 tablespoons passata

dressed green salad, to serve (optional)

· Make up the pizza base mix according to the instructions on the packet. Turn out the dough on a lightly floured surface and knead for 1–2 minutes until smooth. Divide the dough into 4 pieces and knead each a little to form smooth, round balls. Roll each out to a circle about 15 cm (6 inches) across.

· Mix together the chicken, cherry tomatoes, salami, parsley and passata and spoon the filling evenly into the centre of the 4 dough circles. Lightly brush the edges of each circle with a little water and then fold one side over to meet the other. Press together to form 4 pasty shapes. Place on a baking sheet and bake at the top of a preheated oven, 220°C (425°F), Gas Mark 7, for 15 minutes or until pale golden. Serve with a simple green salad dressed with olive oil and balsamic vinegar, if liked.

Smoked Chicken and Salami Wrap

Put 4 tortilla wraps on a board and spread each one with 1 tablespoon sun-dried tomato paste. Arrange 50 g (2 oz) thinly sliced Milano salami over each and scatter each with 25 g (1 oz) smoked chicken. Put 75 g (3 oz) rocket in a bowl with 1 tablespoon olive oil, 1 tablespoon balsamic vinegar and 6 quartered cherry tomatoes and toss well. Put the salad evenly on top of the chicken, roll up tightly and cut each wrap in two, securing with a cocktail stick. Serve cold.

Savoury Smoked Crêpes

Make 100 g (3½ oz) batter mix according to the instructions on the packet. Heat a pancake pan until hot and grease with a little oil. Pour ¼ of the pancake batter into the pan and cook for about 1 minute, flip and cook on the other side for a few seconds until golden. Repeat using the remaining batter to make 4 pancakes. Put 150 ml (¼ pint) passata in a pan with 125 g (4 oz) chopped Milano salami, 125 g (4 oz) chopped smoked chicken and 8 halved cherry tomatoes.

Heat for 2–3 minutes until piping hot then use the mixture to fill the crêpes, folding them in triangles or rolling them up. Place in a shallow, ovenproof dish in a single layer and scatter over 50 g (2 oz) grated Parmesan cheese. Put under a preheated hot grill for 1–2 minutes or until golden. Serve with a simply dressed green salad.

Piri-Piri Stir-Fry

Serves 4

2 tablespoons olive oil
500 g (1 lb) chicken mini-fillets
thyme sprigs, to garnish

For the piri-piri sauce

1 teaspoon minced red chilli
1 teaspoon minced garlic
¼ teaspoon dried oregano
¼ teaspoon dried thyme
1 teaspoon paprika
2 tablespoons red wine vinegar

To serve

express rice
green salad

- Heat the oil in a large, heavy-based wok or frying pan and cook the chicken over a high heat, stirring occasionally, for 5 minutes or until golden in places.

- Meanwhile, mix together all the ingredients for the piri-piri sauce and add to the pan with the chicken. Stir-fry for a further 3–4 minutes, stirring occasionally, until the sauce flavours the chicken and the chicken is cooked through. Garnish with fresh thyme sprigs.

- Serve hot with express rice and a crisp green salad.

Piri-Piri Chicken and Pepper Kebabs

Cut 3 chicken breasts, each about 150 g (5 oz), into cubes and 1 large red pepper into chunks. Thread on to 8 bamboo or metal skewers and place on a foil-lined grill rack. Mix together 2 tablespoons olive oil, 1 teaspoon minced garlic, 1 teaspoon minced chilli, ½ teaspoon dried oregano and ¼ teaspoon dried thyme to make a paste. Add 1 teaspoon paprika and 1 tablespoon red wine vinegar and mix again. Brush the paste over the kebabs. Heat a griddle pan and cook the kebabs over a high heat for 2–3 minutes on each side until golden and lightly charred in places.

Piri-Piri Chicken Thighs with

Griddled Peppers Make 2 deep slashes in 8 chicken thighs. Place them on a preheated griddle pan and cook for 5 minutes on each side. Meanwhile, mix together 1 finely chopped red chilli, 3 tablespoons olive oil, 1 finely chopped or crushed garlic clove, ½ teaspoon dried oregano, the grated rind and juice of 1 lemon, 1 teaspoon paprika and 2 tablespoons red wine vinegar. Put the chicken thighs in a roasting tin and liberally brush with the marinade, then roast at the top of a preheated oven, 200°C (400°F), Gas Mark 6, for 15 minutes. Meanwhile, cut a red pepper into strips and cook, turning occasionally, on the griddle pan for 5 minutes until softened and cooked. Serve the chicken with the peppers and garnished with thyme sprigs.

3️⃣ Quick Coq au Vin

Serves 4

2 tablespoons olive oil
8 chicken drumsticks
8 streaky bacon rashers,
 roughly chopped
8 whole shallots
250 g (8 oz) chestnut
 mushrooms, halved
1 tablespoon plain flour
2 tablespoons thyme leaves
300 ml (½ pint) red wine
450 ml (¾ pint) rich chicken stock
thyme sprigs, to garnish
mashed potatoes, to serve

- Heat the oil in a large, heavy-based frying pan and cook the drumsticks and bacon over a high heat for 5 minutes. Add the shallots and mushrooms and cook for a further 5 minutes, turning the chicken and shallots, until golden all over. Add the flour and toss to coat, then add the thyme.

- Pour in the wine and stock and bring to the boil, stirring continually to distribute the flour evenly within the sauce. Reduce the heat and simmer, uncovered, for 15 minutes until the chicken is cooked through.

- Garnish the coq au vin with thyme sprigs and serve ladled on to hot mashed potatoes in warmed serving bowls.

1️⃣ Chicken, Mushroom and Red Wine Soup with Croutons

Heat 1 tablespoon olive oil in a pan and cook 175 g (6 oz) diced chicken with 1 chopped onion and 125 g (4 oz) roughly chopped mushrooms for 5 minutes over a high heat. Meanwhile, make 40 g (1¾ oz) red wine sauce according to the instructions on the packet and add to the chicken with 300 ml (½ pint) chicken stock. Bring to the boil, ladle into warmed serving bowls and serve scattered with ready-made croutons.

2️⃣ Coq au Vin Style Chicken Breasts

Heat 1 tablespoon olive oil in a large, heavy-based frying pan and cook 4 chicken breasts, each about 125 g (4 oz), and 1 small sliced red onion for 10 minutes, turning the chicken once. Meanwhile, in a separate pan heat 1 tablespoon olive oil and cook 4 rashers of chopped streaky bacon and 175 g (6 oz) halved chestnut mushrooms over a high heat for 5 minutes. Add the mushrooms and bacon to the pan with the chicken. Stir in 150 ml (¼ pint) red wine and 300 ml (½ pint) rich chicken stock and bring to the boil. Reduce the heat, cover and simmer for 5 minutes. Blend 1 teaspoon cornflour with 1 tablespoon water, add to the sauce and stir well to thicken. Serve on a bed of instant mashed potatoes.

30 Chicken, Porcini Mushroom and Pâté Pies

Serves 4

40 g (1½ oz) dried porcini
   mushrooms, chopped
250 g (8 oz) ready-rolled puff
   pastry
beaten egg, to glaze
4 chicken breasts, each about
   125 g (4 oz)
125 g (4 oz) Ardennes pâté
25 g (1 oz) butter
150 ml (¼ pint) white wine
150 ml (¼ pint) double cream
2 tablespoons chopped parsley,
   to garnish

- Soak the porcini mushrooms in 150 ml (¼ pint) boiling water for 10 minutes.

- Cut the puff pastry into 4 diamond shapes and make 3 small incisions in the top. Place on a baking sheet, brush with beaten egg and cook in a preheated oven, 200°C (400°F), Gas Mark 6, for 12–15 minutes until golden and puffed.

- Meanwhile, make large slits in the side of each chicken breast. Cut the pâté into 4 slices and put a slice inside each chicken breast. Divide the mushrooms in half. Put a quarter of one half inside each chicken breast and tie with string. Heat the butter in a large frying pan and cook the chicken breasts over a high heat for 5 minutes on each side until golden.

- Pour in the white wine and remaining mushrooms and bring to the boil. Reduce the heat, turn over the chicken breasts, cover and simmer for 5 minutes. Remove the chicken from the pan and place on 4 warmed serving plates. Add the cream to the pan, heat for 1 minute and spoon over the chicken. Place a pastry top on each and garnish with chopped parsley.

---

1 Hot Chicken, Mushroom and Pâté Wraps with Rocket

Heat 3 tablespoons olive oil in a large frying pan and cook 2 thinly sliced chicken breasts together with 175 g (6 oz) quartered chestnut mushrooms for 7–8 minutes or until golden. Spread 4 flour tortillas each with 25 g (1 oz) pâté and top each with a handful of rocket leaves. Scatter over the hot chicken and mushrooms and roll up tightly. Cut each in half to serve.

2 Chicken Breasts with Mushroom Sauce and Walnut Bread Tops

Pour 150 ml (¼ pint) boiling water over 25 g (1 oz) porcini mushrooms and set aside for 10 minutes. Heat 2 tablespoons olive oil and cook 4 chicken breasts, each about 125 g (4 oz), over a high heat for 5 minutes on each side. Add 175 g (6 oz) quartered chestnut mushrooms and the drained, chopped porcini mushrooms and 150 ml (¼ pint) white wine. Bring to the boil, reduce the heat, cover and simmer for 5 minutes. Meanwhile, grill 4 slices of walnut bread under a hot grill until crisp on both sides. Transfer the chicken breasts to warmed serving plates. Add 8 tablespoons double cream to the pan and bring to a boil. Spoon the sauce over the chicken and top each one with a toasted walnut bread slice.

CHI-FOOD-HAE

Garlic and Herb Stuffed Chicken wit Sun-Blush Tomatoes and Prosciutto

Serves 4

4 chicken breasts, each about
125 g (4 oz)
8 sun-blush tomatoes
125 g (4 oz) garlic and herb
soft cheese
8 slices of prosciutto
3 tablespoons olive oil
8 tablespoons white wine
pepper

- Make a deep cut in the side of each chicken breast, almost cutting them in half widthways, and fill each one with a quarter of the garlic and herb soft cheese and 2 sun-blush tomatoes. Press together and wrap tightly with 2 slices of prosciutto to hold together.

- Heat the oil in a large, heavy-based frying pan and cook the chicken, seam side down, over a high heat for 3–4 minutes on each side or until golden. Add the wine to the pan, cover with a tight-fitting lid and cook for a further 5 minutes or until tender. Serve the chicken on warmed serving plates, well seasoned with pepper and with any juices spooned over.

 Garlic and Herb Chicken with Sun-Blush Tomatoes and Rice
Heat 2 tablespoons olive oil in a large, heavy-based frying pan and cook 375 g (12 oz) diced chicken over a high heat for 7–8 minutes or until golden and cooked through. Add 125 g (4 oz) sun-blush tomatoes to the pan and toss. Mix 200 g (7 oz) garlic and herb soft cheese with 8 tablespoons milk and add to the pan. Heat gently, stirring continually with a wooden spoon, for 1–2 minutes until hot but not boiling. Serve with express rice or instant mash.

Garlic and Herb Chicken en Papilotte Make a deep cut in the side of each of 4 chicken breasts, each about 125 g (4 oz), and fill each with about 25 g (1 oz) garlic and herb soft cheese and 2 sun-blush tomatoes. Wrap each in 2 slices of prosciutto and place each on a piece of kitchen foil. Scrunch up the foil around the chicken a little to form a tray and pour 3 tablespoons white wine into each tray. Slice 1 onion and scatter over the chicken. Wrap the foil up and over to form a parcel. Transfer to a roasting tin and cook in a preheated oven, 200°C (400°F), Gas Mark 6, for 20 minutes, unwrapping the foil for the final 5 minutes of cooking to allow the prosciutto to brown a little. Serve with green beans and mash.

CHI-FOOD-WAS

20 Sweet Balsamic Chicken with Pan-Fried Onions

Serves 4

6 tablespoons balsamic vinegar
4 chicken breasts, each about
   150 g (5 oz)
2 tablespoons olive oil
1 onion, thinly sliced
1 red onion, thinly sliced
2 tablespoons clear honey
1 tablespoon chopped rosemary
150 ml (¼ pint) chicken stock
pepper

To serve
mashed potatoes
green beans

- Put the balsamic vinegar in a bowl and season with pepper. Make 3 small cuts in the top of each of the chicken breasts. Add the chicken to the vinegar and toss to coat. Set aside for 3–4 minutes.

- Meanwhile, heat the oil in a large, heavy-based frying pan and cook the onions over a moderately high heat for 5 minutes or until soft and beginning to turn golden. Add the chicken, cut side down, and cook for 3 minutes. Turn and cook for a further 3 minutes.

- Turn once more and add the balsamic vinegar from the bowl together with the honey and rosemary. Reduce the heat, add the stock, cover and simmer, stirring once, for 3–4 further minutes or until the chicken is cooked through. Serve the chicken on warmed serving plates with the onions spooned over. Serve with mashed potatoes and green beans.

 Balsamic Chicken Bruschetta

Thinly slice 2 chicken breasts, each about 125 g (4 oz), and put in a bowl with 3 tablespoons balsamic vinegar, 1 tablespoon clear honey and ½ teaspoon dried rosemary. Toss together. Heat 1 tablespoon olive oil in a large frying pan and cook the chicken over a high heat for 7–8 minutes until golden and cooked through. Meanwhile, slice 8 large mushrooms and add to the pan for the final 4 minutes of cooking. Lightly toast 4 diagonal slices of ciabatta, spoon the balsamic chicken and mushroom over the top of each slice and serve warm.

 Sweet Balsamic Chicken with Roasted Butternut and Peppers Toss 350 g (11½ oz) ready-prepared butternut squash pieces and 1 red pepper, cut into chunks, with 2 tablespoons olive oil and 2 tablespoons chopped parsley. Toss 2 chicken breasts, each about 125 g (4 oz), with 4 tablespoons balsamic vinegar and 1 tablespoon clear honey. Put the chicken and vegetables in a roasting tin and cook at the top of a preheated oven, 220°C (425°F), Gas Mark 7, for 20 minutes or until golden in places and cooked through. Scatter the chicken and vegetables with 1 tablespoon chopped rosemary leaves and serve with creamy mashed potato, if liked.

CHI-FOOD-BYH

3 Harissa Chicken

Serves 4

3 tablespoons olive oil
1 large onion, roughly chopped
3 chicken breasts, each about
 150 g (5 oz), sliced
½ teaspoon ground cinnamon
1 teaspoon ground cumin
1 teaspoon ground coriander
2 tablespoons harissa
400 g (13 oz) can chopped
 tomatoes
150 ml (¼ pint) hot chicken stock
400 g (13 oz) can chickpeas,
 rinsed and drained
couscous, to serve (optional)

· Heat the oil in a large, heavy-based wok or frying pan and cook the onion and chicken over a high heat for 5 minutes. Add the spices and cook, stirring, for 2 minutes.

· Add the harissa and continue to cook for 2 further minutes before adding the chopped tomatoes and stock. Bring to the boil, reduce the heat, cover and gently simmer for 15 minutes, stirring occasionally.

· Add the drained chickpeas and cook for a further 2 minutes until piping hot. Serve with couscous fluffed with a drizzle of olive oil, if liked.

1 Harissa Chickpea Dip with Chicken

Heat 1 tablespoon olive oil in a frying pan and cook 1 chopped onion and 1 small, roughly chopped chicken breast over a high heat for 5 minutes or until golden and soft. Add 1 tablespoon harissa, ½ teaspoon ground cumin and ½ teaspoon ground coriander. Add 400 g (13 oz) can rinsed and drained chickpeas and 4 tablespoons water. Heat for a further 2 minutes, then transfer to a food processor or blender and process until smooth. Transfer to a serving bowl and serve with breadsticks and sugar snap peas to dip.

2 Yogurt and Harissa Chicken Kebabs

Cut 3 chicken breasts, each about 150 g (5 oz), into cubes and put them in a bowl with 4 tablespoons natural yogurt, 1 tablespoon harissa, a pinch each of cinnamon, cumin and coriander and 2 tablespoons chopped fresh coriander. Toss well to coat the chicken. Thread on to 4 bamboo skewers and place on a foil-lined grill rack with 175 g (6 oz) cherry tomatoes. Grill the kebabs and cherry tomatoes, turning once, for 8–10 minutes or until lightly charred and cooked through. Serve with couscous.

Chicken with a Tarragon Cream Sauce and Mushroom Rice

Serves 4

250 g (8 oz) easy-cook rice

25 g (1 oz) butter

4 chicken breasts, each about (150 g (5 oz), cut diagonally into 6 slices

1 teaspoon Dijon mustard

2 tablespoons tarragon wine vinegar or white wine vinegar

400 ml (14 fl oz) crème fraîche

4 tablespoons chopped tarragon

4 tablespoons olive oil

300 g (10 oz) chestnut mushrooms sliced

1 tablespoon wholegrain mustard

pepper

- Cook the rice in a large saucepan of lightly salted boiling water for 15 minutes or until tender. Drain and set aside.

- Heat the butter in a large, heavy-based frying pan and cook the chicken slices over a high heat for 10 minutes or until golden. Add the Dijon mustard and stir. Add the wine vinegar and stir again, cooking for a few seconds until the vinegar burns off. Pour in the crème fraîche and chopped tarragon, reduce the heat and stir well for 2 minutes until piping hot but not boiling. Season generously with pepper and set aside.

- Meanwhile, heat the oil in a large, heavy-based frying pan and cook the sliced mushrooms over a high heat for 5 minutes or until golden and cooked. Add the drained rice and wholegrain mustard and stir-fry together for 2 minutes until piping hot. Serve the rice spooned on to warmed serving plates with the chicken spooned over.

Warm Chicken, Tarragon and Mushroom Salad Cut 3 chicken breasts, each about 150 g (5 oz), into thin slices. Heat 2 tablespoons olive oil in a pan and cook the chicken with 125 g (4 oz) quartered chestnut mushrooms over a high heat for 5 minutes or until golden and cooked through, adding 2 tablespoons chopped tarragon for the final 1 minute of cooking. Put 2 x 150 g (5 oz) spinach and watercress salad in a serving bowl, add the hot chicken and mushrooms and toss. Flavour a small quantity of mayonnaise with chopped tarragon and serve alongside the warm salad.

Baked Chicken Breasts with Tarragon Sauce Cut a slit in the side of 4 chicken breasts and insert a sprig of tarragon in each. Place in a roasting tin, season generously with salt and pepper and put a knob of butter on top of each. Roast in a preheated oven, 200°C (400°F), Gas Mark 6, for 20–25 minutes or until golden and cooked through. Meanwhile, make the sauce. Heat 25 g (1 oz) butter in a small saucepan, add 25 g (1 oz) plain flour and cook for a few seconds. Remove the pan from the heat and add 2 tablespoons tarragon wine vinegar. Gradually add 300 ml (½ pint) milk a little at a time. Return the pan to the heat and bring to the boil, stirring continually, until the sauce has boiled and thickened. Add 4 tablespoons chopped tarragon and 50 g (2 oz) grated Cheddar cheese. Stir well to melt the cheese and add 6 tablespoons double cream. Serve the chicken with the hot sauce spooned over and with asparagus and new potatoes.

30 Quick Paella with Artichokes, Chorizo and Green Beans

Serves 4

2 tablespoons olive oil

4 chicken drumsticks

75 g (3 oz) chorizo, thinly sliced

1 small red onion, thinly sliced

200 g (7 oz) paella rice

900 ml (1½ pints) rich chicken stock

pinch of saffron threads

400 g (13 oz) can artichoke hearts, drained and halved

100 g (3½ oz) large peeled prawns

100 g (3½ oz) green beans, trimmed

- Heat the oil in a large paella pan, wok or frying pan and cook the chicken drumsticks, turning occasionally, over a high heat for 5 minutes or until golden. Add the chorizo and onion to the chicken and cook, stirring, for 2 minutes.

- Add the rice and toss to mix. Pour in all the stock and the saffron threads and bring to the boil. Reduce the heat, cover and simmer, stirring occasionally, for 15 minutes.

- Add the artichokes, prawns and beans and stir well. Continue to cook, covered, for a further 5 minutes until all the ingredients are piping hot, cooked through and tender.

 Chicken, Artichoke and Green Bean Bruschetta Slice 4 thick diagonal slices from a ciabatta loaf and put them on a foil-lined grill rack. Drizzle each with 1 tablespoon olive oil. Toast under a preheated hot grill for 30 seconds on each side until golden and crisp. Keep warm. Place 300 ml (½ pint) passata in a small saucepan with 400 g (13 oz) can artichoke hearts, halved, a sliced cooked chicken breast and 50 g (2 oz) frozen green beans and bring to the boil. Reduce the heat, cover and simmer for 3–4 minutes until piping hot. Stir through 3 tablespoons chopped parsley and serve on the warm ciabatta toasts.

 Chicken, Prawn and Chorizo Pilaff Cook 250 g (8 oz) easy-cook white rice in a large saucepan of lightly salted boiling water for 12–15 minutes or until tender, then drain. Meanwhile, heat 3 tablespoons olive oil in a large frying pan and cook 1 sliced red onion and 250 g (8 oz) diced chicken meat with 75 g (3 oz) sliced chorizo for 8–10 minutes or until golden. Add 400 g (13 oz) can artichokes, drained and halved, 100 g (3½ oz) frozen peas and 150 ml (¼ pint) chicken stock. Bring to the boil and cook for 2 minutes. Add the drained rice and toss together. Serve in warmed serving bowls with chopped parsley to garnish, if liked.

Chicken Topped with Blue Cheese and Mango Chutney

Serves 4

4 chicken breasts, each about 125 g (4 oz)

1 tablespoon olive oil

4 slices Gorgonzola cheese, each about 25 g (1 oz)

4 generous tablespoons mango chutney

salt and pepper

salad, to serve

- Put the chicken breasts between 2 sheets of clingfilm and beat them with a rolling pin until almost doubled in size and halved in thickness. Season with salt and pepper.

- Brush the chicken breasts with oil and cook, turning once, in a preheated griddle pan for 7–8 minutes or until golden and cooked through.

- Place on 4 warmed serving plates and top each with a slice of Gorgonzola and 1 tablespoon of mango chutney. Serve with a simple salad.

 Griddled Chicken Breasts with Blue Cheese Sauce Put 4 chicken breasts, each about 125 g (4 oz), between 2 sheets of clingfilm and beat with a rolling pin until halved in thickness. Cook the chicken in a hot griddle pan over a high heat, turning once, for 7–8 minutes or until golden and cooked through. Meanwhile, melt 25 g (1 oz) butter in a saucepan, add 25 g (1 oz) plain flour and cook for a few seconds. Remove from the heat and stir in 300 ml (½ pint) milk, a little at a time. Return to the heat and bring to the boil, stirring until boiled and thickened. Remove from the heat and add 125 g (4 oz) crumbled Danish blue or Stilton cheese and stir until melted. Stir in 1 tablespoon thyme leaves and serve the chicken with the sauce spooned over each portion.

Baked Chicken Breasts with Spicy Mangoes and Blue Cheese Use a sharp knife to slice 4 chicken breasts, each about 125 g (4 oz), almost in half along their length. Cut ¼ mango into thin slices and toss with 2 tablespoons mango chutney. Spoon the mixture into the 4 chicken breasts so they are completely full. Wrap each with 2 slices of prosciutto to hold it tightly together and keep the filling intact. Heat 1 tablespoon olive oil in a large, heavy-based frying pan and fry the chicken, turning once, over a high heat for 5 minutes or until pale golden on each side. Transfer to a roasting tin and bake in a preheated oven, 200°C (400°), Gas Mark 6, for 20 minutes until golden and cooked through, placing a thick slice of Gorgonzola cheese, about 40 g (1¾ oz), on the top of each for the final 5 minutes of cooking. Serve with a simple salad, if liked.

CHI-FOOD-NEN

30 Chicken, Apricot and Almond Tagine

Serves 4

1 tablespoon olive oil

1 large onion, chopped

8 boneless, skinless chicken thighs, cut into chunks

1 teaspoon ground cinnamon

1 cinnamon stick

1 teaspoon ground cumin

1 teaspoon ground coriander

½ teaspoon paprika

175 g (6 oz) dried apricots

175 g (6 oz) dried prunes

600 ml (1 pint) chicken stock

1 teaspoon cornflour

5 tablespoons chopped coriander

50 g (2 oz) toasted blanched almonds

couscous, to serve (optional)

- Prepare the couscous, if using, by pouring over warm water according to the instructions on the packet. Set aside.

- Meanwhile, prepare the tagine. Heat the oil in a large, heavy-based saucepan and cook the onion and chicken over a high heat for 5 minutes until golden and beginning to soften. Add all the spices and cook, stirring, for 2 minutes.

- Add the dried fruit and stock. Bring to the boil then reduce the heat to a gentle simmer and cook, uncovered, for a further 15 minutes or until the chicken is tender and the dried fruit soft yet still retaining its shape.

- Blend the cornflour with 1 tablespoon of water and stir into the tagine to thicken. Add the chopped coriander and almonds, stir and heat for a further 1 minute before serving with couscous, if using.

 Quick Couscous Salad with Moroccan Flavours Prepare 110 g (3½ oz) lemon- and coriander-flavoured couscous to the packet instructions. Heat 1 tablespoon olive oil in a large frying pan and cook 2 thinly sliced boneless, skinless chicken thighs, each about 150 g (5 oz), over a high heat for 3–4 minutes. Add 1 bunch roughly chopped spring onions and cook for a further 4 minutes or until the chicken is golden. Add to the couscous with 4 tablespoons chopped coriander, 75 g (3 oz) chopped dried apricots and 50 g (2 oz) toasted flaked almonds.

 Moroccan-Style Chicken Soup Heat 1 tablespoon olive oil in a pan and cook 1 chopped onion and 2 sliced boneless, skinless chicken thighs, each about 125 g (4 oz), over a high heat for 5 minutes or until golden. Add 1 teaspoon each ground cinnamon, ground cumin, ground coriander and paprika and cook, stirring, for a further 1 minute. Add 400 g (13 oz) can chopped tomatoes and 600 ml (1 pint) chicken stock and bring to the boil. Reduce the heat and simmer for 10 minutes before transferring to a food processor or blender. Blend, in batches if necessary, until almost smooth. Return to the pan with 400 g (13 oz) can rinsed and drained chickpeas and 3 tablespoons chopped fresh coriander. Heat through for 2 minutes before ladling into warmed soup bowls and serving with crusty bread.

30 Roast Beetroot, Butternut Wedges and Thyme Thighs

Serves 4

4 boneless chicken thighs

850 g (1¾ lb) ready-prepared butternut squash wedges

300 g (10 oz) raw beetroot (unpeeled), washed and cut into thin wedges

4 tablespoons olive oil

6 unpeeled garlic cloves

about 12 thyme sprigs

salt and pepper

- Open out each of the chicken thighs and season well with salt and pepper.

- Put the butternut squash and beetroot in a large roasting tin and drizzle with the oil. Toss together with the garlic cloves and 8 of the thyme sprigs and season well. Put the remaining 4 thyme sprigs in the centre of each of the boned chicken thighs, roll up and secure with cocktail sticks.

- Roast in a preheated oven, 220°C (425°F), Gas Mark 7, for 20–25 minutes or until the chicken is golden and cooked through and the vegetables are tender; the beetroot should still have a little bite. Serve hot with crusty buttered bread, if liked.

1 Chicken, Beetroot and Cucumber Salad with Thyme Dressing

Cut 300 g (10 oz) cooked beetroot into thin wedges, put them in a bowl with 75 g (3 oz) watercress and toss. Cut ½ cucumber in half, cut into chunks and add to the salad with 250 g (8 oz) flavoured chicken slices (such as tikka) and drizzle with 5 tablespoons thyme-infused olive oil or 5 tablespoons olive oil mixed with 1 teaspoon dried thyme. Season and serve.

2 Chicken, Sweet Potato and Thyme Cannelloni

Heat 2 tablespoons olive oil in a large, heavy-based frying pan and cook 375 g (12 oz) minced chicken and 1 small chopped onion over a high heat for 5 minutes. Add 1 finely chopped sweet potato and 2 tablespoons chopped rosemary leaves and cook for a further 5 minutes or until the potato is beginning to soften. Spoon the mixture evenly on to 8 sheets of fresh lasagne, roll up and place in a shallow, ovenproof dish. Pour over 300 g (10 oz) ready-made cheese sauce and scatter with 50 g (2 oz) grated Parmesan cheese. Place under a preheated hot grill for 3–4 minutes until golden and bubbling.

Chicken Breasts with Crème Fraîche and Three-Mustard Sauce

Serves 4

4 chicken breasts, each about
   150 g (5 oz)
1 tablespoon olive oil
15 g (½ oz) butter
200 ml (7 fl oz) crème fraîche
1 tablespoon wholegrain mustard
1 teaspoon English mustard
1 teaspoon Dijon mustard
3 tablespoons chopped parsley
pepper

To serve

green beans
new potatoes

- Heat the oil and butter in a large, heavy-based frying pan and cook the chicken, turning once, over a high heat for 15 minutes or until golden and cooked through. Use a fish slice to remove the chicken from the pan and keep it warm.

- Add the crème fraîche to the pan with the mustards and stir for 2–3 minutes until warm but not boiled. Stir in the chopped parsley and season generously with pepper. Serve the chicken on warmed serving plates and spoon the sauce over. Serve with green beans and buttered new potatoes, if liked.

 Creamy Chicken Pan-Fry with Hot Mustard Sauce Heat 25 g (1 oz) butter in a pan and cook 375 g (12 oz) diced chicken over a high heat for 7–8 minutes or until golden. Add 1 tablespoon Dijon mustard, 2 teaspoons English mustard and 1 teaspoon wholegrain mustard. Stir well, then add 150 ml (¼ pint) double cream, Stir and heat for 2 minutes until piping hot. Spoon on to warmed serving plates and garnish with parsley sprigs.

 Chicken and Mustard Lattice Pies Line a large baking sheet with baking parchment. Unroll 375 g (12 oz) ready-rolled puff pastry and cut the sheet in half along its length. (Keep the other half for use another time.) Cut half the pastry into 16 long strips, then cut each of these in half widthways. Use each of the 8 strips to make 4 crisscross lattice patterns on the baking sheet. Lightly brush with the beaten egg and bake in a preheated oven, 220°C (425°F), Gas Mark 7, for 15 minutes until golden and crisp.

Meanwhile, heat 25 g (1 oz) butter in a large, heavy-based frying pan and cook 500 g (1 lb) diced chicken over a high heat for 15 minutes until golden and cooked through. Add 200 ml (7 fl oz) crème fraîche, 1 tablespoon wholegrain mustard, 1 teaspoon English and 1 teaspoon Dijon mustard and season generously with pepper. Heat through for 2–3 minutes until piping hot but not boiling. Add 3 tablespoons chopped parsley and stir through. Serve the filling spooned on to warmed serving plates and place a lattice pastry on top of each to serve.

30 Asparagus and Pine Nut Filled Chicken with Mustard Sauce

Serves 4

4 chicken breasts, each about
125 g (4 oz)
12 trimmed fine asparagus stems,
halved lengthways
2 tablespoons toasted pine nuts
2 tablespoons olive oil
15 g (½ oz) butter
400 ml (14 fl oz) crème fraîche
2 tablespoons Dijon mustard
salt and pepper

- Place the chicken breasts on a board and cut them almost in half lengthways. Lay 6 asparagus stems in each and scatter the pine nuts evenly among them. Season generously with salt and pepper, then close each breast and tie with string to hold in place.

- Heat the oil and butter in a large, heavy-based frying pan and cook the chicken over a moderately high heat for 7–8 minutes on each side or until golden and cooked through, covering the pan for the final 5 minutes of cooking.

- Meanwhile, mix together the crème fraîche and Dijon mustard and season well. Spoon into the pan with the chicken and gently heat, stirring, for 2 minutes or until hot. Serve the chicken with the mustard sauce spooned over, accompanied with cooked leeks and soya beans, if liked.

10 Grilled Chicken, Asparagus and Pine Nuts in a Spinach Salad

Slice 2 chicken breasts and put in a bowl with 1 bunch of roughly chopped asparagus. Drizzle with 4 tablespoons olive oil and season generously with salt and pepper. Transfer to a large, foil-lined grill rack and cook under a preheated hot grill for 7–8 minutes or until the chicken is cooked and the asparagus lightly charred and tender. Toss in a bowl with 200 g (7 oz) spinach leaves and 4 tablespoons toasted pine nuts. Drizzle with balsamic vinegar to serve.

20 Creamy Chicken, Asparagus and Pine Nut Tagliatelle

Cook 250 g (8 oz) dried tagliatelle in a large saucepan of lightly salted boiling water for 10 minutes or until tender. Thinly slice 2 chicken breasts, each about 150 g (5 oz). Heat 3 tablespoons olive oil in a large, heavy-based frying pan and cook the chicken over a high heat for 5 minutes or until beginning to brown. Add 1 roughly chopped bunch of asparagus and pan-fry for a further 5 minutes. Add 400 ml (14 fl oz) crème fraîche and 2 tablespoons Dijon mustard and heat, stirring, for 3–4 minutes. Drain the pasta and toss into the pan with the chicken.

QuickCook
Healthy
Feasts

Recipes listed by cooking time

10

Chicken Laksa with Noodles

Serves 4

1–2 tablespoons Thai red curry
  paste
1 litre (1¾ pints) hot chicken stock
300 g (10 oz) cooked chicken,
  torn into strips
375 g (12 oz) ready-cooked thin
  rice noodles
400 ml (14 fl oz) can reduced-fat
  coconut milk
300 g (10 oz) prepared stir-fry
  vegetables
juice of 1 lime
small handful of fresh coriander
salt and pepper

- Fry the curry paste in a large pan for 1 minute. Add the hot stock, chicken and noodles and simmer for 3 minutes.

- Add the coconut milk, bring back to the boil and stir in the prepared stir-fry vegetables. Simmer for 2 minutes, stir in the lime juice and season with salt and pepper. Ladle into bowls and scatter fresh coriander over the top.

2 Stir-Fried Chicken Noodles

Heat 1 tablespoon vegetable oil in a large frying pan and add 3 chicken breasts, each 150 g (5 oz), cut into strips, 1 bunch of spring onions cut into strips, 125 g (4 oz) mangetout and 1 red pepper, cut into strips. Stir-fry over a high heat for 6–7 minutes, then add 1–2 tablespoons Thai red curry paste and 2 × 150 g (5 oz) packs ready-cooked noodles. Heat through and sprinkle with chopped peanuts to serve.

3 Thai Chicken Curry

Chop 3 skinless chicken breast fillets into pieces and stir-fry with 1–2 tablespoons Thai red curry paste and 1 tablespoon vegetable oil for 5 minutes. Add 500 ml (17 fl oz) chicken stock and simmer for 10 minutes before adding 400 ml (13 fl oz) can coconut milk and 300 g (10 oz) prepared stir-fry vegetables. Garnish with fresh coriander leaves and serve with jasmine rice.

20 Chicken Tacos

Serves 4

1 tablespoon vegetable oil
500 g (1 lb) chicken mince
2 garlic cloves, crushed
30 g (1½ oz) taco or fajita
 seasoning mix
juice of 1 lime
8 taco shells

To serve

tomato salsa
fat-free Greek yogurt
shredded crisp lettuce
grated reduced-fat Cheddar
 cheese
lime wedges

- Heat the oil in a frying pan, add the chicken mince and stir-fry, keeping the meat in clumps. Add the garlic and seasoning mix and continue cooking for 5 minutes, adding a little water if the mixture becomes too dry. Stir in the lime juice.

- Warm the taco shells according to the instructions on the packet. Spoon in the mince mixture and top with tomato salsa, yogurt, shredded lettuce and grated cheese, with lime wedges on the side.

10 Tex–Mex Chicken and Beans

Fry 500 g (1 lb) chicken mince in 1 tablespoon sunflower oil over a high heat with 30 g (1½ oz) taco or fajita seasoning mix for 5 minutes until clumpy and cooked. Add 250 ml (8 fl oz) passata and 220 g (7½ oz) can kidney beans, rinsed and drained. Heat through and serve on thick slices of toast from a crusty loaf.

30 Mexican Chicken Burgers with Sweet Potato Wedges

Cut 2 sweet potatoes into thin wedges, toss in 1 tablespoon olive oil, season and spread over a baking sheet. Cook in a preheated oven, 220°C (425°F), Gas Mark 7, turning occasionally, for 25 minutes or until tender. Meanwhile, mix 500 g (1 lb) chicken mince with 1 crushed garlic clove and 30 g (1½ oz) taco or fajita seasoning mix. Shape into 4 burgers and fry in 1 tablespoon oil for 8–10 minutes, turning once, or until browned and cooked through. Serve with tomato salsa, yogurt, crisp lettuce and the sweet potato wedges.

CHI-HEAL-NIO

30 Chicken Drumstick Jambalaya

Serves 4

1 tablespoon sunflower oil

8 chicken drumsticks, skinned

1 onion, chopped

2 garlic cloves, crushed

2 celery sticks, sliced

1 red chilli, deseeded and chopped

1 green pepper, cored, deseeded and chopped

75 g (3 oz) chorizo sausage, sliced

250 ml (8 fl oz) American long grain rice

500 ml (17 fl oz) chicken stock

1 bay leaf

3 tomatoes, cut into wedges

dash of Tabasco sauce

salt and pepper

- Heat the oil in a large pan. Cut a few slashes across the thickest part of the drumsticks, add them to the pan and fry over a high heat for 5 minutes, turning occasionally. Add the onion, garlic, celery, chilli and pepper and cook for a further 2–3 minutes or until softened.

- Add the chorizo, fry briefly, then add the rice, stirring to coat the grains in the pan juices. Pour in the stock, add the bay leaf and bring to the boil. Cover, reduce the heat and simmer for 20 minutes, stirring occasionally, until the stock has been absorbed and the rice is tender.

- Stir in the tomatoes and Tabasco sauce and season to taste. Heat through for 3 minutes before serving.

 Quick Chicken and Chorizo Stew

Pour 350 g (11½ oz) ready-made tomato and roasted pepper pasta sauce into a saucepan. Add 200 g (7 oz) chopped cooked chicken, 75 g (3 oz) sliced chorizo and 400 g (13 oz) can butter beans. Simmer for 5 minutes and serve with crusty bread.

2 Spanish Chicken with Spicy Potatoes Fry 4 skinless chicken breast fillets, cut into chunks, in 1 tablespoon olive oil with 1 sliced onion, 2 crushed garlic cloves, 2 sliced celery sticks and 75 g (3 oz) sliced chorizo sausages. Cook for 5 minutes, stirring. Add 220 g (7½ oz) can chopped tomatoes and a dash of Tabasco sauce and simmer for 10 minutes. Meanwhile, in a separate pan, fry 400 g (13 oz) can of new potatoes, drained and halved, in 1 tablespoon olive oil for 5 minutes or until golden. Add ½ teaspoon smoked paprika and ¼ teaspoon cayenne pepper and cook for 2 minutes. Serve with the Spanish chicken.

30 Griddled Chicken with Coriander Aïoli

Serves 4

2 teaspoons coarsely crushed
black peppercorns
4 skinless chicken breast fillets,
thinly sliced
1 tablespoon olive oil

For the coriander aïoli

small bunch of coriander, leaves
only
1 garlic clove, peeled
2 teaspoons Dijon mustard
1 egg yolk
2 teaspoons white wine vinegar
150 ml (¼ pint) sunflower oil
salt and pepper

- Make the coriander aioli. Reserve a few coriander leaves for garnish and place the rest in a small food processor or blender with the garlic, mustard, egg yolk and vinegar. Blend until finely chopped. With the motor running, slowly drizzle in the oil until the mixture is smooth and thick. Season with salt and pepper.

- Scatter the crushed peppercorns over the chicken slices and drizzle with oil. Cook, in batches, on a preheated hot griddle for 1–2 minutes on each side or until cooked through and golden.

- Serve the warm chicken slices with mixed green salad leaves, grated beetroot and the coriander aïoli. Garnish with the reserved coriander leaves.

 Griddled Chicken and Tomato Sandwiches Thinly slice 3 skinless chicken breast fillets, season with salt and plenty of pepper and drizzle with 1 tablespoon olive oil. Cut 4 tomatoes in half, season and drizzle with a little oil. Cook the chicken and tomatoes, in batches, on a preheated hot griddle for 1–2 minutes on each side until cooked and golden. Sandwich between slices of crusty granary bread with rocket leaves and ready-made roast garlic mayonnaise.

 Griddled Chicken with Garlic Mayonnaise Thinly slice 4 skinless chicken breast fillets, sprinkle with 2 teaspoons coarsely crushed black peppercorns and drizzle over 1 tablespoon olive oil. Cook, in batches, on a preheated hot griddle for 1–2 minutes each side or until cooked through and golden. Stir 1 crushed garlic clove into 150 ml (¼ pint) ready-made reduced-fat mayonnaise. Serve with mixed green salad leaves.

Chicken Minestrone

Serves 4

400 g (13 oz) can chopped
    tomatoes
600 ml (1 pint) chicken stock
125 g (4 oz) cooked chicken,
    chopped
1 courgette, chopped
125 g (4 oz) mixed frozen
    vegetables
75 g (3 oz) mini-pasta shapes
1 tablespoon ready-made pesto
salt and pepper

- Put the tomatoes, stock, chicken, courgette and frozen vegetables in a saucepan. Bring to the boil, stirring, then add the pasta shapes and simmer for 5 minutes until the pasta is just tender.

- Season with salt and pepper and stir in the pesto just before serving.

Vegetable Chicken and Rice

Put 400 g (13 oz) can chopped tomatoes in a saucepan with 200 g (7 oz) chopped cooked chicken, 1 chopped courgette, 125 g (4 oz) frozen mixed vegetables and 125 ml (¼ pint) chicken stock and heat. Simmer for 5 minutes, add 250 g (8 oz) long grain rice and simmer, stirring occasionally, for 10 minutes or until the rice is cooked, adding a little boiling water if the mixture is too dry. Stir in 125 g (4 oz) baby spinach leaves until just wilted.

Chicken and Vegetable Casserole

Cut 4 boneless, skinless chicken breast fillets in half lengthways and fry in 1 tablespoon olive oil until browned on both sides. Add 400 g (13 oz) can chopped tomatoes, 1 chopped courgette and 200 g (7 oz) frozen mixed vegetables. Cover and simmer gently for 15 minutes, stir in 2 tablespoons ready-made pesto and serve with cooked tagliatelle.

30 Chicken and Aubergine Bake

Serves 4

1 aubergine, thinly sliced

olive oil spray

6 skinless chicken thigh fillets, chopped

350 g (11½ oz) ready-made tomato and basil pasta sauce

150 g (5 oz) mozzarella cheese, drained and chopped

50 g (2 oz) fresh white breadcrumbs

2 tablespoons freshly grated Parmesan cheese

salt and pepper

- Place the aubergine slices on a foil-lined grill pan and lightly spray with oil. Grill for about 5 minutes, turning once, or until tender.

- Meanwhile, lightly spray a nonstick frying pan with oil and cook the chicken over a high heat for 5 minutes or until cooked through. Stir in the pasta sauce and bring to the boil.

- Place half the aubergine slices in the base of an ovenproof dish, pour the chicken and tomato mixture over the top and cover with the remaining aubergine. Mix together the mozzarella, breadcrumbs, Parmesan and seasoning and sprinkle over the top. Bake in a preheated oven, 200°C (400°F), Gas Mark 6, for 15 minutes until the topping is golden and crisp.

 Chicken, Aubergine and Tomato Soup Stir-fry 4 chopped skinless chicken thigh fillets in 1 tablespoon olive oil with 1 chopped aubergine for 5 minutes. Stir in 600 ml (1 pint) ready-made tomato soup and heat through until hot. Serve with a swirl of low-fat yogurt.

 Chicken and Aubergine Spaghetti Fry 1 chopped aubergine and 1 chopped courgette in 1 tablespoon sunflower oil with 4 chopped skinless chicken thigh fillets for 5 minutes. Add 350 g (11½ oz) ready-made tomato and basil pasta sauce, bring to the boil and simmer for 10 minutes. Meanwhile, cook 250 g (8 oz) spaghetti in lightly salted boiling water for 10 minutes or until cooked. Drain, add to the tomato mixture with 2 tablespoons chopped parsley. Serve with a little freshly grated Parmesan cheese.

30 Chicken Pilau with Cauliflower, Spinach and Green Beans

Serves 4

1 tablespoon sunflower oil

1 onion, chopped

6 skinless chicken thigh fillets, chopped

2 tablespoons korma curry paste

250 ml (8 fl oz) basmati rice (measured in a measuring jug)

1 litre (1¾ pints) chicken stock

1 small cauliflower, cut into florets

150 g (5 oz) frozen leaf spinach

125 g (4 oz) green beans, trimmed and halved widthways

2 carrots, coarsely grated

25 g (1 oz) flaked almonds, toasted

salt and pepper

low-fat natural yogurt, to serve

- Heat the oil in a large pan. Add the onion and chicken and cook, stirring, for 5 minutes. Stir in the curry paste, rice, stock, cauliflower and green beans. Bring to the boil, reduce the heat, cover and simmer for 10 minutes until the stock has been absorbed and the rice and vegetables are tender.

- Stir in the grated carrot, heat through for 1 minute, season with salt and pepper, sprinkle with flaked almonds and serve with natural yogurt.

---

10 Curried Chicken and Rice

Heat 2 tablespoons korma paste in a pan, add 200 g (7 oz) chopped cooked chicken, 200 g (7 oz) frozen mixed vegetables and about 4 tablespoons boiling water. Cover and cook for 5 minutes, stir in 500 g (1 lb) ready-cooked pilau rice and heat through for 3 minutes, stirring, until hot.

20 Creamy Chicken Curry with Cauliflower and Spinach

Fry 1 chopped onion, 6 chopped skinless chicken thigh fillets and 1 small cauliflower, cut into florets, in 1 tablespoon sunflower oil for 5 minutes. Add 125 g (4 oz) sliced mushrooms, 150 ml (¼ pint) chicken stock and 2 tablespoons mild curry paste. Simmer for 5 minutes, then stir in 150 g (5 oz) low-fat Greek natural yogurt. Stir well, season with salt and pepper and heat through. Add 75 g (3 oz) baby spinach leaves and stir until wilted. Serve with rice or naan bread.

CHI-HEAL-TOX

30 Lime and Sweet Chilli Chicken with Sweet Potato Mash

Serves 4

3 sweet potatoes, chopped
1 tablespoon sweet chilli sauce
1 tablespoon soy sauce
2 tablespoons lime juice
4 skinless chicken breast fillets,
   halved horizontally
2 teaspoons sesame oil
1 tablespoon sesame seeds
25 g (1 oz) reduced-fat spread
skimmed milk, to mix
salt and pepper
green beans, to serve

- Cook the sweet potatoes in a large saucepan of lightly salted boiling water for 15–20 minutes or until tender.

- Meanwhile, in a large, shallow dish mix together the sweet chilli sauce, soy sauce and lime juice. Add the chicken breast halves and turn to coat in the mixture.

- Heat the sesame oil in a large, nonstick frying pan, add the chicken and fry for 5 minutes on each side, turning once, or until browned and cooked through. Add any remaining sauce mixture and sprinkle in the sesame seeds. Cook for a few more minutes.

- Drain the sweet potatoes and mash with the reduced-fat spread and a little milk until smooth. Season with salt and pepper. Serve with the sweet chilli chicken and accompanied with green beans.

 Sticky Chilli Chicken Lettuce Wraps

Toss 410 g (13½ oz) chicken mini-fillets in 2 tablespoons sweet chilli sauce. Stir-fry in 2 teaspoons sesame oil for 5 minutes until cooked. Add a squeeze of lime juice and serve with crisp lettuce leaves to wrap the chicken. Serve with extra sweet chilli sauce separately for dipping.

 Lime and Sweet Chilli Chicken Salad

Cut 4 skinless chicken breast fillets into strips and toss in a mixture of 1 tablespoon sweet chilli sauce, 1 tablespoon soy sauce and 2 tablespoons lime juice. Stir-fry in 2 teaspoons sesame oil for 5 minutes. Serve on a bed on crisp shredded lettuce, thinly sliced cucumber and a handful of roughly chopped fresh coriander.

CHI-HEAL-XOS

Chicken Couscous Salad

Serves 4

250 g (8 oz) couscous
250 ml (8 fl oz) hot chicken stock
400 g (13 oz) can chickpeas, drained
200 g (7 oz) roasted peppers in oil from a jar, drained and chopped; with 3 tablespoons oil reserved
125 g (4 oz) cherry tomatoes, halved
4 tablespoons chopped mixed herbs, such as parsley, mint and fresh coriander
200 g (7 oz) cooked barbecue-flavoured chicken, chopped
1 tablespoon white wine vinegar
1 teaspoon Dijon mustard
salt and pepper

- Put the couscous in a heatproof bowl, pour over the hot stock, cover the bowl with clingfilm and leave to stand for 5–8 minutes until the stock has been absorbed.

- Meanwhile, in a large bowl mix together the chickpeas, peppers, tomatoes, herbs and chicken.

- In a small bowl mix together the oil from the peppers, the vinegar and mustard. Season with salt and pepper. Uncover the couscous, fluff up with a fork, add the dressing and chicken mixture and stir well to mix.

Pasta Salad

Cook 250 g (8 oz) pasta shapes in lightly salted boiling water for 10 minutes or until just tender. Drain, rinse under cold water and drain again. Add 125 g (4 oz) halved cherry tomatoes, 3 tablespoons chopped mixed herbs, 125 g (4 oz) roasted peppers from a jar and 200 g (7 oz) cooked chopped barbecue-flavoured chicken. Mix together with 4 tablespoons ready-made French dressing, 50 g (2 oz) black olives and a handful of rocket leaves.

Stuffed Peppers

Halve and deseed 4 red peppers and roast in a preheated oven, 220°C (425°F), Gas Mark 7, for 20 minutes until softened and lightly charred. Meanwhile, soak 175 g (6 oz) couscous in 175 ml (6 fl oz) hot chicken stock for 10 minutes or until the stock has been absorbed. Fluff up with a fork and stir in 125 g (4 oz) halved cherry tomatoes, 3 tablespoons chopped mixed parsley, mint and coriander, 175 g (6 oz) chopped cooked barbecue-flavoured chicken and 75 g (3 oz) chopped haloumi cheese. Spoon the mixture into the pepper halves, drizzle with a little olive oil and finish under the grill for 5 minutes to brown.

3⦿ Saucy Lemon Chicken with Greens

Serves 4

2 teaspoons sesame oil
4 skinless chicken breast fillets
1 red chilli, deseeded and chopped
finely grated rind of 1 lemon
8 tablespoons lemon juice
2 heads of pak choi, halved
1 tablespoon cornflour, mixed to a
    paste with 2 tablespoons water

- Heat the sesame oil in a large, heavy-based frying pan, add the chicken breasts and fry, turning once, for 5 minutes or until browned. Add the chilli to the pan with the lemon rind and juice. Cover and simmer for 15 minutes or until the chicken is cooked.

- Meanwhile, steam or lightly cook the pak choi in a little lightly salted boiling water until just tender.

- Remove the chicken from the pan and keep warm. Stir the cornflour paste into the pan juices and bring to the boil, stirring until thickened and adding a little water if the sauce is too thick. Serve the chicken with the pak choi and the lemon sauce poured over the top.

1⦿ Lemon Noodle Chicken

Stir-fry 200 g (7 oz) chicken mini-fillets in 2 teaspoons sesame oil for 5 minutes or until browned and cooked. Add 75 g (3 oz) lemon stir-fry sauce, 300 g (10 oz) prepared mixed stir-fry vegetables and 150 g (5 oz) ready-cooked noodles. Cook, stirring, for 5 minutes and serve.

2⦿ Pineapple Chicken

Stir-fry 4 skinless chicken breast fillets cut into strips in 1 teaspoon sesame oil for 5 minutes or until golden and cooked. Drain 220 g (7½ oz) can pineapple pieces in natural juice, reserving the juice. Add the pineapple, 1 deseeded and chopped red chilli and 2 heads of pak choi, leaves separated, to the pan. Cook for 3 minutes until hot. Mix a little of the reserved pineapple juice with 1 tablespoon cornflour to make a smooth paste, then stir in the remaining juice. Pour into the pan and cook, stirring, until thickened. Serve with noodles.

CHI-HEAL-HUH

Spanish Chicken and Potato Stew

Serves 4

2 tablespoon olive oil

4 boneless, skinless chicken thighs, thinly sliced

500 g (1 lb) potatoes, cut into small cubes

1 red onion, sliced

1 green pepper, cored, deseeded and thinly sliced

1 small red chilli, roughly chopped

1 garlic clove, crushed

1 tablespoon smoked paprika

400 g (13 oz) can chopped tomatoes

3 large tomatoes, roughly chopped

300 ml (½ pint) chicken stock

salt and pepper

crusty bread, to serve

- Heat the oil in a pan, add the chicken, potatoes, onion, green pepper, chilli, garlic and paprika and cook, stirring, over a high heat for 10 minutes.

- Add the canned tomatoes, fresh tomatoes and stock and bring to the boil, then reduce the heat and simmer, uncovered, for 6–7 minutes or until the chicken and potatoes are cooked through and the tomatoes have softened. Season with salt and pepper and serve with crusty bread to mop up the juices.

Chicken and Chorizo Pasta

Fry 6 chopped boneless skinless chicken thigh fillets with 125 g (4 oz) sliced chorizo for 3 minutes over a high heat. Stir in 350 g (11½ oz) ready-made tomato and chilli pasta sauce and simmer for 5 minutes. Meanwhile, cook 375 g (12 oz) tagliatelle in a large saucepan of lightly salted boiling water. Drain the tagliatelle, add the sauce, stir well and serve.

Chilli Chicken

Chop 8 boneless skinless chicken thigh fillets and fry in 1 tablespoon olive oil with 1 chopped onion, 1 chopped green pepper and 2 teaspoons chilli powder for 5 minutes. Add 1 tablespoon tomato purée with 400 g (13 oz) can cannellini beans, rinsed and drained, and 400 g (13 oz) can chopped tomatoes. Make a tomato salsa by mixing 2 chopped tomatoes, 1 small chopped red onion and 1 tablespoon chopped parsley. Serve the chicken with the salsa, rice and fat-free Greek yogurt.

Mixed Mushroom, Herb and Chicken Frittata

Serves 4

1 tablespoon olive oil

1 skinless chicken breast fillet, sliced

200 g (7 oz) mixed mushrooms, such as chestnut, oyster and shiitake, sliced

1 red pepper, cored, deseeded and chopped

4 spring onions, sliced

8 eggs

3 tablespoons chopped herbs, such as parsley, chives and thyme

125 g (4 oz) low-fat soft cheese with chives

salt and pepper

- Heat the oil in a large, nonstick frying pan. Add the chicken, mushrooms, red pepper and spring onions and cook over a high heat, stirring, for 5 minutes or until the chicken is cooked and the vegetables are tender.

- Beat the eggs with the herbs and season with salt and pepper. Pour into the pan over the chicken and vegetables and cook gently for about 5 minutes or until set around the edges.

- Dot the soft cheese over the top of the frittata and place the pan under a medium grill. Cook until the frittata is just set and the top is golden. Serve warm or cold.

---

1 Garlic Mushroom and Chicken Pizza

Fry 200 g (7 oz) sliced mixed mushrooms in 1 tablespoon sunflower oil for 3 minutes, then stir in 1 chopped cooked chicken breast. Spread a ready-made pizza base with pizza topping sauce, spoon the mushroom mixture over the top and dot with low-fat garlic and herb soft cheese. Grill until melted and golden.

30 Pasta Bake

In a large frying pan, fry 2 sliced skinless chicken breast fillets in 1 tablespoon sunflower oil with 200 g (7 oz) mixed sliced mushrooms, 1 chopped red pepper and 4 chopped spring onions. Stir in 125 g (4 oz) low-fat soft cheese with chives and 200 ml (7 fl oz) reduced-fat crème fraîche. Heat to make a sauce, adding a little hot water if too thick.

Season with salt and pepper, add 3 tablespoons chopped mixed herbs and stir in 250 g (8 oz) cooked pasta shapes. Tip into a heatproof dish, sprinkle with a little freshly grated Parmesan cheese and grill for 5 minutes until golden.

30 Baked Chicken and Prawn Spring Rolls

Serves 4

200 g (7 oz) prepared mixed stir-fry vegetables

1 tablespoon sesame oil

1 red chilli, deseeded and chopped

1 cm (½ inch) piece fresh ginger, grated

200 g (7 oz) cooked chicken, chopped

125 g (4 oz) small peeled prawns, thawed if frozen, chopped

2 tablespoons Chinese stir-fry sauce, any flavour

6 sheets filo pastry

2 tablespoons sunflower oil

salt and pepper

teriyaki sauce, for dipping

- Roughly chop the stir-fry vegetables to make the pieces slightly smaller, then place in a bowl. Add the sesame oil, chilli, ginger, chicken, prawns and sauce. Season with salt and pepper and mix well.

- Work with 1 sheet of filo pastry at a time and keep the rest covered with clingfilm to prevent it from drying out. Cut each sheet in half widthways and put one-twelfth of the chicken mixture at one end of each strip. Roll it up, tucking in the ends as you roll. Place on a baking sheet and brush with a little sunflower oil. Repeat with remaining pastry and filling to make 12 rolls.

- Bake in a preheated oven, 200°C (400°F), Gas Mark 6, for 15 minutes until golden and crisp. Serve warm with teriyaki sauce for dipping.

 Teriyaki Chicken Rolls

Warm 12 pancakes (the sort used for crispy duck) in the microwave according to the instructions on the packet. Fill with 250 g (8 oz) cooked chicken cut into strips, 6 spring onions, cut into fine strips and ¼ cucumber, cut into sticks. Top with a little teriyaki sauce, roll up and serve.

 Chicken and Prawn Filo Tarts

Brush 4 sheets of filo pastry with a little sunflower oil, fold each sheet in half widthways and scrunch the edges roughly to make a circle with a ruffled edge. Place on two baking sheets, brush with a little more oil and bake in a preheated oven, 200°C (400°F), Gas Mark 6, for 10 minutes or until golden and crisp.

Meanwhile, stir-fry 200 g (7 oz) prepared mixed stir-fry vegetables, 1 chopped red chilli, 1 cm (½ inch) piece ginger, grated, 200 g (7 oz) chopped cooked chicken and 125 g (4 oz) peeled prawns in 1 tablespoon vegetable oil. Add 2–3 tablespoons teriyaki sauce and heat through. Spoon into the filo tart cases and drizzle with a little extra teriyaki sauce to serve.

30 Chicken Ratatouille

Serves 4

8 small, skinless chicken thighs
1 tablespoon olive oil
1 onion, chopped
1 aubergine, cut into bite-sized
  chunks
1 green pepper, cored, deseeded
  and cut into bite-sized chunks
1 red pepper, cored, deseeded
  and cut into bite-sized chunks
2 courgettes, chopped
1 garlic clove, crushed
400 g (13 oz) can chopped
  tomatoes
pinch of caster sugar
handful of basil leaves, roughly
  torn
salt and pepper

- Cut a couple of slashes across each chicken thigh and season with salt and pepper. Heat the oil in a large deep frying pan, add the chicken and cook over a high heat for 5 minutes, turning occasionally.

- Add the onion, aubergine, peppers, courgettes and garlic and cook for 10 minutes or until softened, adding a little water if the mixture becomes too dry.

- Add the tomatoes and sugar, season with salt and pepper and bring to the boil, stirring. Reduce the heat, cover and simmer for 15 minutes, stirring occasionally. Stir in the basil and serve.

 Chicken Ratatouille Pie Heat 2 × 420 g (14 oz) cans ratatouille in a saucepan. Add 250 g (8 oz) chopped cooked chicken, heat through and tip into a heatproof dish. Scatter over ½ ciabatta loaf torn into pieces and sprinkle with 2 tablespoons freshly grated Parmesan cheese. Grill for a few minutes until the bread is toasted.

 Chicken Ratatouille with Lentils Chop 4 boneless skinless chicken breasts and fry in 1 tablespoon olive oil for 5 minutes. Add 1 chopped aubergine, 2 chopped courgettes, 2 chopped roasted red peppers from a can or jar, 400 g (13 oz) can chopped tomatoes with garlic and herbs and 400 g (13 oz) can green lentils, rinsed and drained. Bring to the boil, reduce the heat, cover and simmer for 10 minutes. Sprinkle with chopped basil before serving.

Chicken Tikka Kebabs with Red Onion Relish

Serves 4

150 ml (5 fl oz) low-fat natural yogurt

2 tablespoons tandoori or tikka paste

4 tablespoons lemon juice

4 skinless chicken breast fillets, cut into bite-sized pieces

1 red onion, finely sliced

2 tablespoons chopped fresh coriander

1 tablespoon olive oil

basmati rice, to serve

- Mix together the yogurt, tandoori or tikka paste and half the lemon juice. Add the chicken and stir well. Thread on to skewers and place on a foil-lined grill pan.

- Cook under a preheated hot grill, turning occasionally, for 8–10 minutes or until the chicken is cooked and lightly charred at the edges.

- Meanwhile, make the relish by mixing together the red onion, fresh coriander, oil and remaining lemon juice. Serve with the chicken tikka and rice.

Chicken Tikka Wraps

Put pieces of cooked chicken tikka on a soft flour tortilla, top with shredded spring onion, crisp lettuce and cucumber sticks. Spoon on some ready-made tzatziki and roll up.

Chicken Tikka Masala

Prepare the chicken as above. While it is cooking make the masala sauce. Fry 1 chopped onion in 1 tablespoon oil, add 1 crushed garlic clove, 1 teaspoon ground cumin, 1 teaspoon ground coriander and 1½ teaspoons garam masala. Stir in 400 g (13 oz) can chopped tomatoes and simmer for 10 minutes. Remove from the heat and stir in 150 g (5 oz) fat-free Greek yogurt. Reheat gently but do not boil. Take the cooked chicken tikka off the skewers and stir into the sauce. Serve with red onion relish and rice.

CHI-HEAL-NAC

 # Spiced Roast Chicken with Lime

Serves 4

8 small chicken thighs, skinned
1 tablespoon harissa
4 tablespoons clear honey
2 limes, cut into wedges
1 red pepper, cored deseeded
  and cut large chunks
2 courgettes, cut into chunks
1 onion, cut into wedges
300 g (10 oz) new potatoes,
  halved if large
1 tablespoon olive oil
salt and pepper

- Cut a few slashes across each chicken thigh. Mix together the harissa and honey and rub all over the chicken thighs. Place in a roasting tin large enough to spread everything out in a single layer, with the lime wedges, red pepper, courgettes, onion and potatoes.

- Drizzle over the oil, season with salt and pepper and roast in a preheated oven, 220°C (425°F), Gas Mark 7, for 25 minutes, turning occasionally, or until the chicken is cooked and the vegetables are tender. Serve with the juice of the lime wedges squeezed over the chicken.

 ### Harissa Chicken Pittas

Coat 410 g (13½ oz) chicken mini-fillets in 1 tablespoon harissa and 1 tablespoon clear honey. Stir-fry in 1 tablespoon sunflower oil for 5 minutes until cooked through. Pile into warmed pitta bread with shredded crisp lettuce, grated carrot and spoonfuls of ready-made reduced-fat hummus.

 ### Pan-Fried Spicy Chicken

Cut 8 small skinless chicken thigh fillets into strips and coat in a mixture of 1 tablespoon harissa and 1 tablespoon clear honey. Heat 1 tablespoon sunflower oil in a large frying pan, add the chicken and fry over a medium heat for 5 minutes. Add 1 deseeded and chopped pepper, 2 chopped courgettes, 1 onion, cut into thin wedges, and 2 limes, cut into wedges. Cook for 10 minutes, stirring occasionally, or until the chicken is cooked and the vegetables are tender. Serve with new potatoes.

30 Coconut and Coriander Chicken

Serves 4

1 tablespoon sunflower oil

4 skinless chicken breast fillets

1 bunch of spring onions, chopped

150 ml (¼ pint) reduced-fat coconut milk

1 tablespoon nam pla (Thai fish sauce)

juice of 1 lime

1 teaspoon cornflour

small handful of fresh coriander leaves, roughly chopped

handful of coconut shavings

salt and pepper

To serve

Thai sticky rice

mangetout

• Heat the oil in a large frying pan, add the chicken breasts and cook, turning once, for 5 minutes or until browned. Remove the chicken from the pan and slice, then return to the pan. Add the spring onions, coconut milk, fish sauce and lime juice. Season with salt and pepper, cover the pan and simmer gently for 20 minutes or until the chicken is cooked.

• Mix the cornflour with 1 tablespoon water and add to the sauce to thicken if necessary. Stir in half the coriander leaves and sprinkle the rest over the top with the coconut shavings. Serve with Thai sticky rice and mangetout.

---

10 Coconut, Coriander and Chicken Salad

Mix 300 g (10 oz) sliced cooked chicken with 2 handfuls of fresh coriander leaves, 125 g (4 oz) bean sprouts, 125 g (4 oz) mangetout, a handful of coconut shavings and ¼ chopped cucumber. Drizzle over 4 tablespoons reduced-fat ready-made Thai-style salad dressing before serving.

20 Coconut and Coriander Chicken Soup

Heat 400 ml (14 fl oz) reduced-fat coconut milk with 500 ml (17 fl oz) chicken stock. Add 3 chopped skinless chicken breasts, 2 tablespoons Thai fish sauce, 1 bunch of chopped spring onions and a handful of roughly chopped fresh coriander leaves. Simmer for 15 minutes. Add the juice of 1 lime, season with salt and pepper and serve sprinkled with coconut shavings and extra coriander leaves.

Warm Chicken, Pine Nut and Raisin Salad

Serves 4

2 tablespoons pine nuts

4 skinless chicken breast fillets, halved horizontally

2–3 teaspoons paprika

1 tablespoon olive oil

handful of radicchio leaves

100 g (3½ oz) mixed salad leaves

1 red onion, thinly sliced

4 tablespoons sherry vinegar

2 teaspoons Dijon mustard

2 tablespoons clear honey

50 g (2 oz) raisins

salt and pepper

· Heat a nonstick frying pan until hot. Add the pine nuts and dry-fry, stirring continuously, until golden, taking care not to let them burn. Tip them out of the pan on to a plate.

· Lightly dust the chicken breast halves with paprika and season with salt and pepper. Heat the oil in the pan and fry the chicken breasts, turning occasionally, for about 10 minutes or until cooked through.

· Meanwhile, mix together the radicchio, salad leaves and red onion and place on serving plates. Remove the chicken from the pan and stir the vinegar, mustard and honey into the pan juices. Heat though and add the raisins and pine nuts. Pour the warm dressing over the salad and serve with the chicken.

Paprika Chicken Wraps

Dust 410 g (13½ oz) chicken mini-fillets in 1 teaspoon smoked paprika. Fry in a little olive oil over a high heat for 3 minutes until cooked. Stir in 1 tablespoon sherry vinegar and 1 teaspoon Dijon mustard, season with salt and pepper and pile on to soft tortilla wraps with mixed salad leaves, including peppery rocket or watercress, and thinly sliced red onion. Roll up and serve warm.

Chicken, Raisin and Pine Nut Pilau

Cook 250 g (8 oz) basmati rice in lightly salted boiling water for 10 minutes or according to the instructions on the packet. Cut 4 skinless chicken breast fillets into bite-sized pieces and fry in 1 tablespoon olive oil and 1 teaspoon smoked paprika with 1 thinly sliced red onion for 5 minutes. Add the drained rice with 125 g (4 oz) baby spinach leaves, 2 tablespoons raisins and 2 tablespoons pine nuts. Season and stir well to mix.

3 ⬤ Herby Quinoa with Lemon and Chicken

Serves 4

200 g (7 oz) quinoa
1 tablespoon olive oil
1 onion, chopped
1 garlic clove, crushed
4 skinless chicken breast fillets,
  sliced
1 teaspoon ground coriander
½ teaspoon ground cumin
50 g (2 oz) dried cranberries
75 g (3 oz) no-need-to-soak
  dried apricots, chopped
4 tablespoons chopped parsley
4 tablespoons chopped mint
finely grated rind of 1 lemon
salt and pepper

- Cook the quinoa in a pan of lightly salted boiling water for 15 minutes until tender, then drain.

- Meanwhile, heat the oil in a large frying pan, add the onion and cook, stirring, for 5 minutes to soften. Add the garlic, chicken, coriander and cumin and cook for a further 8–10 minutes until the chicken is cooked.

- Season the quinoa with salt and pepper. Add the chicken mixture, cranberries, apricots, herbs and lemon rind. Stir well and serve warm or cold.

---

1 ⬤ Chicken and Apricot Moroccan Couscous Put 110 g (3½ oz) Moroccan-flavoured couscous in a bowl, cover with boiling water, cover the bowl with clingfilm and leave to stand for 8 minutes. When all the water has been absorbed, stir in 250 g (8 oz) chopped cooked chicken, 125 g (4 oz) no-need-to-soak apricots and 220 g (7½ oz) can chickpeas, rinsed and drained.

2 ⬤ Coriander Couscous with Lemon and Chicken Put 200 g (7 oz) couscous in a bowl, just cover with boiling water, cover the bowl with clingfilm and leave to stand for 10 minutes. Meanwhile, fry 1 chopped onion, 1 crushed garlic clove, and 4 chopped skinless chicken breast fillets in 1 tablespoon olive oil for 10 minutes or until the chicken is cooked. When the couscous has absorbed all the water, fluff it up with a fork, season and stir in the chicken mixture with 4 tablespoons chopped fresh coriander, the grated rind of 1 lemon and 3 tablespoons raisins.

20 Chicken Koftas

Serves 4

500 g (1 lb) chicken mince
2 garlic cloves, crushed
1 teaspoon ground cumin
2 teaspoons ground coriander
2 teaspoons fresh coriander
200 g (7 oz) fat-free
   Greek yogurt
1 tablespoon mint sauce
¼ cucumber, coarsely grated
   and squeezed to remove
   excess liquid
salt and pepper

- Put the chicken mince, garlic, cumin, ground coriander and fresh coriander in a bowl. Season with salt and pepper and mix well.

- Using wet hands, make 12 even-sized sausage shapes from the mixture and thread on to skewers, pressing firmly. Grill for 10 minutes, turning occasionally, until cooked through and browned.

- Meanwhile, mix together the yogurt, mint sauce and cucumber. Take the koftas off the skewers and serve in warmed pitta breads with salad leaves, tomatoes and the yogurt dressing.

10 Spiced Mince with Pitta Bread

Fry 500 g (1 lb) chicken mince in 1 tablespoon sunflower oil over a high heat with 1 teaspoon garlic paste, 1 teaspoon ground cumin, 2 teaspoons ground coriander and 1 teaspoon dried oregano. Add a little water to keep the mixture moist, and 125 g (4 oz) frozen peas. Cook for 8 minutes and serve with warmed pitta bread and ready-made raita or tzatziki.

30 Quick Moussaka

Fry 500 g (1 lb) chicken mince in 1 tablespoon sunflower oil until browned. Add 1 crushed garlic clove, 1 teaspoon ground cumin, 2 teaspoons ground coriander and 400 g (13 oz) can chopped tomatoes. Simmer for 10 minutes. Meanwhile, thinly slice 1 aubergine, brush with a little oil and cook in a hot frying pan for 2 minutes each side. Tip the mince mixture into a baking dish and arrange the aubergine slices on top. Cover with 200 g (7 oz) fat-free Greek yogurt mixed with 1 egg. Put the dish under a medium grill and cook until golden and bubbling. Serve with a green salad.

1 Stir-Fried Chicken with Basil

Serves 2

1 tablespoon vegetable oil

2 shallots, sliced

1 red chilli, deseeded and sliced

1 garlic clove, sliced

375 g (12 oz) chicken mini-fillets

1 tablespoon nam pla (Thai fish sauce)

1 teaspoon soy sauce

small handful of basil leaves

toasted coconut flakes, to garnish (optional)

- Heat the oil in a wok or large frying pan. Add the shallots, chilli and garlic and cook for 1 minute. Remove with a slotted spoon and keep warm.

- Add the chicken to the pan, stir-fry for 5 minutes until cooked and beginning to brown. Return the shallot mixture to the pan, then add the fish sauce, soy sauce and basil and cook for 1 minute until the basil starts to wilt. Sprinkle with toasted coconut flakes, if using, and serve.

2 Chicken and Basil Soup

Place 2 chopped shallots, 1 chopped red chilli, 1 crushed garlic clove and 220 g (7½ oz) chicken mini-fillets in 500 ml (17 fl oz) hot chicken stock. Simmer for 10 minutes, then add 150 g (5 oz) ready-cooked noodles, 1 tablespoon Thai fish sauce, 1 teaspoon soy sauce and a small handful of basil leaves. Simmer for 5 minutes, then sprinkle with toasted flaked coconut and serve.

3 Spring Rolls

Brush 4 sheets of filo pastry with a little oil. Prepare the stir-fried chicken as above and spoon one-quarter of the mixture on to each sheet and roll up to make 4 parcels, tucking the ends in as you go. Brush with a little oil, sprinkle with sesame seeds and bake in a preheated oven, 220°C (425°F), Gas Mark 7, for 10 minutes until crisp and golden. Serve with sweet chilli sauce separately for dipping.

30 Chicken Roasted with Lemon, Olives and Saffron

Serves 4

pinch of saffron threads
4 chicken drumsticks and
4 small chicken thighs, skinned
1 lemon, halved
2 tablespoon clear honey
150 ml (¼ pint) dry white wine
125 g (4 oz) green olives
salt and pepper
2 tablespoons roughly chopped
   flat leaf parsley, to garnish

- Soak the saffron in 1 tablespoon boiling water. Cut a couple of slashes across the top of each piece of chicken and season with salt and pepper. Spread out the chicken in a large roasting tin or ovenproof dish and squeeze over the lemon halves.

- Drizzle over the honey, pour over the saffron threads and soaking water and add the white wine. Roast in a preheated oven, 220°C (425°F), Gas Mark 7, for 20 minutes, basting with the juices occasionally. Add the olives and cook for a further 5 minutes until the chicken is cooked.

- Sprinkle with parsley and serve with new potatoes and green beans.

 Lemon Chicken Stir-Fry

Heat 1 tablespoon sunflower oil in a wok or large frying pan, add 410 g (13½ oz) chicken mini-fillets and stir-fry over a high heat for 5 minutes. Add 1 tablespoon clear honey, 4 tablespoons lemon juice, 4 tablespoons dry white wine and 125 g (4 oz) green olives. Heat through for 2 minutes, season and serve with ready-made couscous salad.

 Roasted Chicken Breasts with Olives and Couscous

Soak a pinch of saffron threads in 1 tablespoon boiling water. Cut 4 skinless chicken breast fillets into 3 pieces each and place them in a roasting tin with 2 halved lemons. Drizzle over 1 tablespoon clear honey, the saffron and soaking water and 150 ml (¼ pint) dry white wine. Season with salt and pepper and roast in a preheated oven, 220°C (425°F), Gas Mark 7, for 15 minutes or until the chicken is cooked. Stir in 125 g (4 oz) green olives, sprinkle with 2 tablespoons chopped parsley and serve with couscous.

 # Yogurt Chicken with Greek Salad

Serves 4

150 g (5 oz) fat-free Greek
  yogurt
1 garlic clove, crushed
2 tablespoons olive oil
finely grated rind and juice of
  1 lemon
1 teaspoon ground cumin
4 skinless chicken breast fillets,
  cut into bite-sized chunks
½ cucumber, chopped
1 red onion, sliced
4 tomatoes, cut into slim wedges
16 black olives
175 g (6 oz) feta cheese,
  crumbled
1 small cos (romaine) lettuce, torn

For the dressing

1 tablespoon lemon juice
2 tablespoons olive oil
1 tablespoon chopped fresh
  oregano or ½ teaspoon dried
  oregano

- Soak 8 small wooden skewers in water and preheat the grill to high. In a bowl, mix together the yogurt, garlic, olive oil, lemon rind and juice and cumin. Add the chicken, stir well and thread on to 8 skewers. Place on a foil-lined grill pan.

- Cook under a preheated hot grill for 10 minutes, turning occasionally, or until the chicken is cooked and beginning to char in places.

- Meanwhile, in a salad bowl mix together the cucumber, onion, tomatoes, olives, feta and lettuce.

- Make the dressing by whisking together the lemon juice, oil and fresh or dried oregano. Pour the dressing over the salad and lightly mix together. Serve with the chicken skewers.

---

1 **Grilled Yogurt Chicken and Spinach Ciabatta** Prepare the chicken skewers as above. Split a ciabatta loaf lengthways and spread with mayonnaise. Top with a handful of baby spinach leaves, a few teaspoons of tomato chilli jam and the hot chicken skewers.

3 **Yogurt Chicken and Bulgar Wheat Salad** Prepare the chicken skewers as above. While they are cooking put 75 g (3 oz) bulgar wheat in a pan with 400 ml (14 fl oz) boiling water. Cover and simmer for 15 minutes until the liquid has been absorbed. Cool slightly before mixing with ½ chopped cucumber, 1 sliced red onion, 4 chopped tomatoes, 16 black olives, 175 g (6 oz) crumbled feta cheese and 2 tablespoons each of chopped parsley and chopped mint.

2 Chicken with Cashews and Oyster Sauce

Serves 2

50 g (2 oz) unsalted cashew nuts
1 teaspoon sesame oil
2 skinless chicken breast fillets,
    cut into strips
1 garlic clove, crushed
1 cm (½ inch) piece fresh ginger,
    grated
125 g (4 oz) oyster mushrooms,
    sliced
4 spring onions, thickly sliced
    diagonally
125 g (4 oz) frozen soya beans
6 tablespoons oyster sauce

• Heat a wok or large frying pan until hot, add the cashew nuts and cook, stirring, for 1 minute or until golden, taking care not to let them burn. Tip them out of the pan on to a plate and set aside.

• Add the oil to the pan with the chicken strips and cook, stirring, for 3 minutes or until browned and cooked through.

• Add the garlic, ginger, mushrooms and spring onions and cook for 2 minutes or until the mushrooms and onions are just tender. Add the soya beans and oyster sauce, bring to the boil and simmer for 2 minutes, adding a little water if the mixture is too dry. Sprinkle over the toasted cashew nuts before serving.

 Ginger Chicken and Rice Stir-Fry

Cook 2 chopped skinless chicken breast fillets in a large frying pan with 1 teaspoon sunflower oil, 1 teaspoon garlic paste, 1 teaspoon ginger paste, 4 sliced spring onions and 125 g (4 oz) frozen soya beans. Add 250 g (8 oz) ready-cooked egg-fried rice and a dash of sweet chilli sauce and soy sauce. Stir-fry until hot.

3 Lemon Chicken with Cashews

Toast 50 g (2 oz) unsalted cashew nuts in a dry frying pan or wok until golden. Remove from the pan, then heat 1 teaspoon sunflower oil and stir-fry 2 skinless chicken breast fillets, cut into strips, for 3 minutes. Add 1 crushed garlic clove, 1 cm (½ inch) piece fresh ginger grated, 1 chopped red chilli, 4 spring onions, sliced diagonally, and 125 g (4 oz) frozen soya beans and fry for 5 minutes. Add 4 tablespoons chicken stock, 4 tablespoons lemon juice, 1 teaspoon soy sauce and 1 teaspoon cornflour mixed to a paste with a little water. Stir until thickened, sprinkle over the cashew nuts and serve.

Index

Page references in *italics* indicate photographs

Acknowledgements

Recipes by Emma Jane Frost
Executive Editor Eleanor Maxfield
Senior Editor Sybella Stephens
Copy Editor Lydia Darbyshire
Art Direction Tracy Killick for Tracy Killick Art Direction and Design
Original design concept www.gradedesign.com
Designer Sally Bond for Tracy Killick Art Direction and Design
Photographer Lis Parsons
Home Economist Emma Jane Frost
Prop Stylist Liz Hippisley
Production Caroline Alberti